CONTENTS

Pages 1-6	How to Diet Delicious	**Pages 11-26**	Breakfast Recipes
Page 7	Baking Protein Powder	**Pages 27-48**	Dessert Recipes
Pages 8-9	Delicious Tips for Success	**Pages 49-69**	Lunch & Dinner Recipes
Page 10	Measurement Conversions	**Pages 70-77**	Side Recipes

TPC

The Protein Chef's Delicious Dieting Volume 1 by **Derek Howes**

"Everything In Moderation"

IMPORTANT LINKS

- Find videos for almost all of my recipes here: **https://theproteinchef.co**

- Find and purchase a majority of the ingredients I use here: **https://theproteinchef.co/ingredients**

- Find and purchase my favorite products (like my food scale) here: **https://theproteinchef.co/products**

CONTACT ME

Have questions or suggestions? Don't ever hesitate to e-mail me at

derek@theproteinchef.co

NEED PROTEIN POWDER?

Buy **The Protein Chef Baking Protein**! My powder has no artificial ANYTHING in it, is gluten AND sugar free, works perfectly with all of my recipes, and is AFFORDABLE (seriously)! **Check it out or purchase at:**

ProteinChefPowder.com

HOW TO DIET DELICIOUS

Delicious Dieting is something that I've created throughout the past decade of training. There is no "**one size fits all**" when it comes to dieting and exercise and it's important to remember that. The tools I give you here should be used as stepping stones to reach your goals. Throughout time you should learn to better understand how your body responds best and progress from there. Some people can function off of a low carb diet and others, like myself, feel like death. Some people respond best to higher reps in a workout and others see better results doing lower reps. Use this protocol as a base and find out what works for you.

PART 1: DIET

I think it's safe to say **everyone at some point has complained about trying to lose weight, gain weight, or put on muscle**. We've all heard about the latest and greatest diets popping up every other month that claim to do what most people have trouble doing, losing those unwanted pounds or packing on some muscle. The thing with all these latest and greatest diets are that 90% of the time it's even EASIER than they make it seem. **Losing weight or gaining muscle is only as hard as you make it**.

There are **two parts to reaching your goals**, diet and exercise. The first and most important part is diet. You can live in the gym but if your diet isn't in-check then you aren't going to make much progress. This is by far the hardest part of any diet. **The concept is simple**:

Eat under your "maintenance" and you WILL lose weight. **Calories out > calories in = weight loss**. Eat over your "maintenance" and you WILL gain weight. **Calories in > calories out = weight gain**.

Lets talk about the magic word "maintenance". Maintenance in terms of dieting, is the amount of calories you need to eat in order to maintain your current weight. By eating **over maintenance you'll gain weight** and by eating **under maintenance you'll lose weight**. Seems simple, right? That's because it is!

Finding out your maintenance is is the hardest part of the equation. The guideline I use for determining maintenance is 13-15 calories per 1 pound of bodyweight. If you are 200 pounds, your maintenance calories would be around 2,600-3,000. Since we all have different metabolisms, bodyfat %, genes, etc, you may or may not need to eat 2,600-3,000 calories to maintain 200 pounds. The baseline of using 13-15 calories per 1 pound of bodyweight is just what you should

1

HOW TO DIET DELICIOUS

start with. To accurately find your maintenance you'll need to weigh yourself in the morning and eat whatever you think your maintenance is for 1 full week. **If your weight stays the same then you have found your maintenance**.

Here is a simple equation that I like to call the **DMA (Delicious Meals ALWAYS) Method**:

10-12xBodyweight to Drop Weight / 13-15xBodyweight to Maintain Weight / 16-18xBodyweight to Add Weight

Once you've found your maintenance **the hardest part is over**. To lose weight, you'll have to eat under your maintenance. The key is to not eat too far under maintenance or you'll do more damage than good. Eating too far under maintenance will hurt your metabolism, cause muscle loss, kill your libido and so on. I recommend losing no more than 1-2 pounds per week depending on how much you weigh. This amount of weight loss will be optimal in saving as much muscle as possible. There are a few exception to this for example if you're extremely overweight or are holding a lot of water you'll tend to drop much more weight than the average person but it'll eventually level off.

To eat under maintenance you simply want to lower your calories by 4-600. If you are 200 pounds and maintaining at 3,000 calories a day then you would want to lower your calories to 2,400-2,600 to effectively lose 1-2 pounds a week. You'll want to check every 2nd week to see if you're still losing weight and adjust accordingly. If weight loss has stalled I recommend dropping your calories by 250-350 and continuing on with the diet. If you're losing an extreme amount of weight then you'll want to add more calories into your diet in order to save as much muscle mass as possible. In this case I would suggest adding 150-200 calories back into your diet.

To gain weight, you'll have to eat over your maintenance. Though most would say gaining weight is easier than losing it I do want to suggest at a max only gaining around 1-2 pounds per week, anything more than that will typically result in a large fat gain. The key is to add on lean muscle which takes much longer than fat.

To eat over maintenance you're going to apply the same rules you did for losing weight but reverse them. Raise your calories by 4-600 and check every 2nd week to see if you're still gaining weight. If you start to notice the pounds coming on quicker than they should then cut your calories back by 1-200 until you're where you want to be.

Something to remember is that 1 pound is 3,500 calories. If you want to lose or gain 1 pound a week with your current exercise level then you'll have to drop or add your calories to 500 below or over maintenance. **500 calories x 7 days = 3,500 calories = 1 pound.**

HOW TO DIET DELICIOUS

Calorie Tips:

- If you want to lose more, lower them more.
- If you want to gain more, add more.
- If you are more active on one day, add more.
- If you are less active on one day, subtract more.
- If you see progress slow down lower your calories by 2-300 or try and be more active.
- A scale is sometimes not the best indicator of fat loss. **You may be losing fat while gaining muscle** aka lowering your bodyfat % so use a mirror and/or pictures to also monitor your progression.

Once you know how many calories to eat the hardest part is done and what you'll eat is what you like **aka DELICIOUS DIETING!** If you can stay with-in your macros (I dive into what macros are below), you will pretty much be able to **eat whatever you want**. No, that doesn't mean you can gorge on unhealthy desserts, fast food, etc. It just simply means that you won't be limited to what foods you can eat. As long as those foods fit with-in your macros you can eat them!

Your macros are your daily intake of **fats, carbs, and protein**.

The standard macro range I have most people follow/see the best results with and suggest YOU start out with is **30% Fat, 35% Carbs, and 35% Protein**. This means that if you are trying to eat 2,500 calories a day:

- 750 calories will come from fat (83.3 grams of fat)
- 750 calories will come from carbs (206 grams of carbs)
- 1,000 calories will come from protein (206 grams of protein)

Good to know:

- 1 gram of protein has 4 calories
- 1 gram of carbohydrates has 4 calories
- 1 gram of fat has 9 calories

The great thing about technology nowadays is that there's no shortage of applications to do just about everything short of working out for you. If you can't track the calories and macros in your head or don't have time to write them all down, use one of the thousand calorie counting computer or phone applications to track them throughout the day. These applications have every food known to man listed, allow you to add whatever macro split you want, and will maybe take you 2 minutes a day to do once you get into the habit of tracking.

HOW TO DIET DELICIOUS

Once you understand what you should be eating and how much of what, you won't need to be as strict with your tracking.

For the most part, **you can eat whatever you want as long as it fits into your macros**. If some days you make room in your macros in order to eat some pizza, it's not going to kill your diet. The key is moderation, common sense, and keeping track of your calories/macros.

Quick tip: You also want to make sure you are drinking enough water. Aside from the various health benefits of consuming water you'll also keep off water weight/bloat (if you don't drink enough your body will retain water/boat).

PART 2: EXERCISE

The second part of the equation: exercising. This is the part that a lot of people over think. The key is to just being consistent. I personally recommend 3-4 days a week with combined cardio and weightlifting for losing weight. **You don't need to spend all day, everyday in the gym to reach your goals**. The type of cardio you do is up to you and should be the type of cardio you prefer doing so that you don't mind doing it! Whether it's swimming, jogging, incline walking, trainers, jump rope, etc…it's all going to do the same thing; burn calories. The weightlifting portion of exercising will help you retain and/or build as much muscle as possible during the diet as well as burn calories.

The type of exercise routine you should do is all dependent on you and what you like. The BEST routine is one that you can stick with, even if it's not the most beneficial. Why? Because you'll stick with it! **There is no perfect routine or exercise for anyone**. Get to know your body and see which routine your body responds best to. I've had clients that saw their greatest results with something I personally saw bad results with. **EVERYONE is different**. You must always keep an open mind and ultimately find out what works best for you. If you hate what you're doing or eating, chances are, you are just setting yourself up to fail.

Delicious Dieting Exercise Program:
Push/Pull/Legs How you incorporate this is completely up to you. Example:

Sun: Push **Mon:** Pull **Tues:** Legs **Wed:** Off/Cardio **Thurs:** Push **Fri:** Pull **Sat:** Legs

Then repeat. You don't need set days, the goal here is to take it by cycles of 3. What I mean by this is that 1 cycle = Push/Pull/Legs, so if it takes you 7 days to complete the 3 workout days then 1 cycle for you is going to be 7 days. If you complete the 3 workouts in 3 days then 1 cycle for you is going to be 3 days…and so on.

HOW TO DIET DELICIOUS

Here is what each specific day will look like. **NOTE:** Whatever your preference is and what you have available is what you should use. Machines, cables, bands dumbbells, benches, or smith machines. Work with what you have!

Push: Flat Chest Press, Incline Chest Press, Chest Fly, Shoulder Press, Lateral Raises, Front Raises, Tricep Push-downs, 1- Arm Tricep Reverse Pushdowns, and Skullcrushers or Closegrip Press (rotate each cycle)

Pull: Max Wide Grip Pull ups you can do in 5 minutes (assisted if needed), 3 sets of Chin ups to failure (assisted if needed), Rack Pulls above the knee, Rows (T-Bar, Dumbbell, or Bent Over), Front Pulldowns, 4 sets of Hyper Extensions to failure, Spider Curls, Hammer Curls, and Concentration Curls.

Legs: Squats, Lunges or Bulgarian Split Squats, 1-Leg Leg Press, 1-Leg Leg Extensions, 1-Leg Leg Curls, and Calf Raises

Abs: 4 sets of Planks (however long you can hold them for), Hanging Leg or Knee Raises (assisted if needed), and L-Sits. **I suggest working out your abs once or twice a week, having a strong core improves everything**.

Cardio: 20-30 minutes, 2-3 times a week of whatever your preferred cardio is. If you're trying to lose weight slowly incorporate more time OR more intense cardio into your routine as time goes on.

Routine Tips:

- Never compromise form! If you're ever in doubt about your form record it, ask someone by you to critique it, or search for tutorials online.
- Can't do an exercise listed? Search for alternatives online!
- Bored with an exercise? Switch it up by using 1-Arm or 1-Leg instead of both and if it calls for 1-Arm or 1-Leg try using both!

As far as your sets and rep ranges here is the rotation of cycles I would do (a cycle is 1 rotation of Push/Pull/Legs, which would be 3 total days):

2 Cycles 8-12 Reps, 1 Cycle 5-8 Reps, 1 Cycles 4-6 Reps, 1 Cycle 13-17 Reps, 2 Cycles 5-8 Reps, 1 Cycle 15-20 Reps

I suggest 1-2 warm-up sets on every exercise and then at least one set as close to max effort as you feel comfortable reaching. Once you reach that set move on to the next exercise.

HOW TO DIET DELICIOUS

Things to take into consideration:

- Don't try and do everything at once. Over-doing it will make you stressed out and will lead to failure. Start by slowly getting rid of junk food, going to the gym once a week, doing cardio at home, and so on. Small changes lead to BIG changes!
- Don't over-think anything. There is so much information and mis-information out there that you could spend years researching a single topic. Keep it simple!
- Don't spend your life in the gym. Your body needs rest to repair itself and for your muscles to grow.

The most important thing I've learned throughout time is that habits make up who we are as a whole. **The absolute most IMPORTANT habit I've learned** is to learn to fall. If you learn to fall then no matter what you're doing, you'll always progress. Say you pickup a skateboard and want to learn to drop-in on a half-pipe, you're already mentally preparing yourself for falling. You get up there, you fall, and you get back up. Each time you fall you naturally learn to take the fall a bit easier, which way to move, how to position yourself for a fall, and so on. Over time you learn to drop in and the rest is history. You'll still fall occasionally but you'll know everything you need to do to get right back at it. With dieting or anything that takes some self-control you don't naturally learn to take falls and rather tend to see it as failure or total loss the second it goes south. What you need to understand is that you WILL fall and you won't stop falling but you can learn to get right back up. You'll miss a workout here and there, you'll miss meals, you'll have a few too many beers, you'll eat bad, you won't drink enough water sometimes, and so on. Is this a big deal? No, not at all. It's only a big deal when you make those things habits, **that's how diets fail**. Rather than looking at messing up as a failure or total loss, learn to create the habit of understanding and moving on. As you do this overtime you'll learn quickly to get back up and onto routine. Learn the process of getting back up and the next time you fall do your best to simplify the process even more. Once you establish healthy habits there's no stopping what you can do in all aspects of your life!

BAKING PROTEIN POWDER

Does heating up protein powder destroy it? Whether baking, microwaving, sunbathing with it, leaving it in a hot car or anything else short of lighting it on fire...the short answer is (drum roll) NO!

Whatever type of protein powder you use whether it's whey, casein, egg, soy, and so on, it's all going to be the same thing. For example, whey protein comes from the by-product of the cheese making process, egg protein is made from pasteurized egg whites that have been dehydrated, soy protein is a protein that is isolated from soybean, and the list goes on. So what is this same thing? **They are all REAL digestible food**. I think some people quickly forget this! It's a supplement so they think that it's some type of magical food that's not real, which isn't the case at all. Protein powder is real food just like chicken that we bake, meals we microwave, and jerky or dehydrated foods we leave in the car. **Heating up protein powder does not destroy it at all**.

Does cooking protein powder denature it at all? First off, denaturing in this aspect, is basically the changing of the protein structure which **YOUR BODY DOES ANYWAYS**. Imagine your protein as a rope with various knots in it and the knots are your amino acids Those knots becoming untied means they are becoming denatured. If the protein powder was a rubix cube and you "denatured" it, then you would essentially be rearranging the colors. In this case, **cooking protein powder DOES denature it**, the structure changes when the protein powder is heated. **Is this bad? No, not at all!** The same thing happens to meat, eggs, soybeans, and so on. Even though the structure has changed, the nutritional value remains the same. If your protein powder is 129 calories per serving with 1 gram of fat, 5 grams of carbs, and 25 grams of protein then it's going to be exactly that even after cooking it. The only factor that's going to change is sometimes digestion. When protein powder is mixed with water, it's going to digest much faster than when baked with something like rolled oats, which takes much longer to digest. At the end of the day **you're not losing ANY nutritional value**. Imagine denaturing is a slinky of amino acids and it becomes untangled. You can still eat the slinky and you're still going to absorb it all (please don't eat a slinky).

Cooking protein powder is 100% safe. If you can bake meats or cook eggs on the stove top, you can without question cook protein powder.

DELICIOUS TIPS FOR SUCCESS

READ ALL OF THESE TIPS BEFORE MAKING ANYTHING! The tips you see below will help you cater the recipes to your liking or needs, save money, and succeed in ANY kitchen that you have access to.

1. Depending on **how powerful your microwave** is, recipes that call for a microwave may take MORE or LESS time. Keep an eye on whatever you're making and once it's done remember how long it took for next time!
2. **Always measure your ingredients for what you're baking**! There are NO shortcuts with baked goods, it's a science!
3. **Switch up your flavors** by using different flavored protein powders!
4. Have access to flavored Greek yogurt? Another way to **switch up your flavors** is by using different flavors, just make sure they compliment the recipe!
5. Too much sugar? **Cut down on the sugar** in a recipe by using the healthiest sugar free alternatives you prefer!
6. **Having trouble finding ingredients locally?** Buy ingredients in bulk online and save money doing so! You can find a ton of the ingredients I use on my website: **https://theproteinchef.co/ingredients**
7. **Purchase all of my favorite products** (hand mixer, blender, food processor, food scale, etc) on my website: **https://theproteinchef.co/products**
8. **Fozen fruit or vegetables** in your shakes or smoothies and you don't need to use as much ice, if any at all!
9. **Make your mix less sticky** by putting it in the fridge for 20 minutes or keeping your hands damp!
10. **Peel a banana even quicker** by pinching the bottom and pulling apart!
11. **Jelly =** made from the juice of the fruit
12. **Jam =** made by crushing the fruit
13. **Look for lower sodium alternatives** to each ingredient if the sodium is too high in a recipe!
14. **Let your cream cheese soften up** before mixing it in, your forearm will thank you!
15. **The easiest way to check** if most things you're baking are done is by inserting a toothpick into the middle of whatever it is you're making and if it comes out clean, it's done!
16. **Make your unflavored protein powder chocolate** by using a couple tablespoons of cocoa powder per scoop used!
17. **Make your unflavored protein powder vanilla** by using 1-2 teaspoons of vanilla extract per scoop used!
18. When in doubt, weigh it out! **The quickest and most accurate way to make any of these recipes** is by using a digital kitchen scale. Did something go wrong with your recipe? Chances are you added too much or too little of something!
19. If the baking dish or pan you're using is big (making your recipe THIN) then it's going to **cook much quicker**. If the baking dish or pan you're using is small (making your recipe THICK) then it's going to take a bit **longer to cook**!

DELICIOUS TIPS FOR SUCCESS

20. If you **use a BAD tasting protein powder** your end result will almost always come out equally as bad as your protein powder!
21. Are **your recipes cooking too fast**? Too slow? Burning? Not at all? Use an oven thermometer to make sure that your oven is calibrated correctly!
22. **Make your own chili seasoning mix** with 2 teaspoon chili powder, 1/2 tablespoon crushed red pepper, 1/2 tablespoon onion powder, 1/2 tablespoon garlic powder, 1 teaspoon sweetener, 1 teaspoon sugar, 1 teaspoon dried parsley, 1 teaspoon salt, 1/2 teaspoon dried basil, and 1/8 teaspoon black pepper!
23. **Make your own taco seasoning mix** with 2 teaspoons chili powder, 1 1/2 teaspoon paprika, 1 teaspoon onion powder, 1/2 teaspoon salt, 1/2 teaspoon garlic powder, 1/2 teaspoon ground cumin, 1/2 teaspoon oregano, and 1/4 teaspoon black pepper!
24. The thicker your batter is, **the thicker your pancakes will be**!
25. **Using a topping for your crepes, pancakes, or waffles**? Make sure that after you put your topping into them that you cover it up with some batter so that it doesn't burn when you flip it over!
26. **Use these recipes as a base**. Feel comfortable replacing ingredients with similar ingredients you like!
27. **Always use sharp knives**. Using a dull knife is dangerous and inefficient.
28. **Parchment paper for baked goods** will make them easier to remove and cleanup a breeze!
29. **If you're using a frosting** make sure you let your recipe cool off a bit before you add it on or it will more than likely immediately melt and slide off!

30. **Practice makes perfect**. Recipes may not come out perfect everytime but everytime you make them you're that much closer to perfecting them all the time!
31. **Use a thermometer to check your meat temperature**! Thermometers are CHEAP and will work great in any environment to keep your meat from overcooking and drying out.
32. **Never use a glass cutting board**! They're slippery, hard to use, and will dull your knives like no other!
33. **Wash your pans and dishes immediately after using them**. Waiting to wash them will only make the process take much longer and could potentially ruin your pan or dish!
34. **Take out and measure all of your ingredients before starting the recipe**. Rushing around could result in injury, a failed recipe, and unneeded stress!
35. **Read the recipe a couple times before starting**. Do it, seriously.

MEASUREMENT CONVERSIONS

Using this conversion chart will help you whether you measure ingredients by volume or by weight

1/16 TEASPOON	=	Dash
1/8 TEASPOON	=	A pinch
1 TEASPOON	=	1/3 Tablespoon or 5 ml
3 TEASPOONS	=	1 Tablespoon or 1/2 Fluid Ounce or 15 ml
1/8 CUP	=	2 Tablespoons or 1 Fluid Ounce or 30 ml
3 TABLESPOONS	=	1 1/2 Fluid Ounces or 1 Jigger
1/4 CUP	=	4 Tablespoons or 2 Fluid Ounces
1/3 CUP	=	5 Tablespoons + 1 Teaspoon
3/8 CUP	=	1/4 Cup + 2 Tablespoons
1/2 CUP	=	8 Tablespoons or 4 Fluid Ounces
3/4 CUP	=	12 Tablespoons or 6 Fluid Ounces
1 CUP	=	16 Tablespoons or 1/2 Pint or 8 Fluid Ounces or 240 ml
1 PINT	=	2 Cups or 16 Fluid Ounces
1 QUART	=	2 Pints or 4 Cups or 32 Fluid Ounces
1 LITER	=	34 Fluid Ounces
1 GALLON	=	4 Quarts or 8 Pints or 16 Cups or 128 Fluid Ounces
1 POUND	=	16 Ounces or 454 Grams
100 GRAMS	=	3.5 Ounces

ALL OF THE...
BREAKFAST RECIPES

11

INGREDIENTS

- 1 1/2 cups (120g) rolled oats
- 2 scoops (60g) vanilla protein powder
- 2 1/2 teaspoons baking powder
- 1/2 teaspoon salt
- 4 teaspoons sweetener
- 1 1/2 teaspoons ground cinnamon
- 1 medium banana
- 1 teaspoon vanilla extract
- 1 large egg or 2 large egg whites
- 1/2 cup (4 ounces) sugar free vanilla coconut milk or milk/other milk substitute
- 1/2 cup (113g) fat free cottage cheese
- 1/4 cup (30g) chopped walnuts or other nuts

HOW TO MAKE THEM

1. Turn your Rolled Oats into oat flour by processing or blending them until they look like flour
2. Add all of your dry ingredients into either your food processor, blender, or large bowl
3. Process, blend, or mix everything together
4. Add in your wet ingredients
5. Lightly process, blend, or mix those in
6. Turn your waffle maker on, let it heat up, and coat it with some non-stick cooking spray
7. Pour your mix in and let it cook for around 2-3 minutes or however long your waffle maker says to

 $1.20   8:00

BANANA NUT WAFFLES

NUTRITION

Whole Recipe
Makes: 1 Recipe
Calories: 1197
Fat: 37g
Saturated Fat: 7g
Sodium: 787mg
Carbs: 123g
Fiber: 19g
Sugar: 29g
Protein: 93g

BREAKFAST BITES

INGREDIENTS

3 large eggs
2 large egg whites
4 tablespoons (20g) grated parmesan cheese
1/4 cup (28g) reduced fat mexican blend cheese or other cheese
1/4 cup (113g) cottage cheese
3 teaspoons (15g) chili sauce
1 tablespoon (7g) bacon bits

HOW TO MAKE THEM

1. Combine all of your ingredients aside from your Bacon Bits into a bowl
2. Mix everything together until it's smooth
3. Take out a large or mini muffin pan and coat it with some non-stick cooking spray
4. Sprinkle your Bacon Bits on top
5. Bake on 350F/176C for 20 minutes

 $1.70   **22:00**

TIP

Change them up by adding in ham, rolled oats, vegetables, sauces, and/or spices!

NUTRITION

Whole Recipe
Makes: 1 Recipe
Calories: 497
Fat: 25g
Saturated Fat: 11g
Sodium: 630mg
Carbs: 9g
Fiber: 0g
Sugar: 8g
Protein: 59g

13

BREAKFAST SKILLET

INGREDIENTS

1 tablespoon olive oil
1 pound (16 ounces) lean ground beef or turkey
8 tablespoons (132g) salsa
1 cup (124g) low sodium pasta sauce
1/2 cup kale or other greens
2 large eggs or 4 large egg whites
1 large egg white
3/4 cup (84g) reduced fat mexican blend cheese or other cheese

HOW TO MAKE IT

1. Take out a skillet, add in your Olive Oil, and brown your Beef
2. Chop up your Kale, turn your burner down to Medium Heat, and add in your your Salsa, Pasta Sauce, and chopped Kale
3. Mix everything together
4. Add in your Eggs and Egg White
5. Let them cook for a couple minutes
6. Sprinkle on your Cheese
7. Let it continue cooking until your cheese is melted

 $3.50   **20:00**

TIP

Add whatever else you want in or ontop of it! Mushrooms, bell peppers, onions, BACON, and so on!

NUTRITION

Whole Recipe
Makes: 1 Recipe
Calories: 1293
Fat: 65g
Saturated Fat: 21g
Sodium: 1452mg
Carbs: 36g
Fiber: 7g
Sugar: 18g
Protein: 141g

1/2 SKILLET
Makes: 1 Skillet
Calories: 646
Fat: 32.5g
Saturated Fat: 10.5g
Sodium: 726mg
Carbs: 18g
Fiber: 3.5g
Sugar: 9g
Protein: 70.5g

COFFEE CAKE

INGREDIENTS

2 cups (160g) rolled oats
1/2 teaspoon salt
2 teaspoons baking powder
4 tablespoons (60g) sugar free chocolate chips
1 1/2 teaspoons ground cinnamon
4 scoops (120g) vanilla protein powder
1/3 cup sweetener
5.3 ounces (150g) fat free plain greek yogurt
1 teaspoon vanilla extract
1 teaspoon caramel extract or 1 tablespoon caramel
3 teaspoons coffee extract or 1 1/2 ounces coffee
2 extra large eggs
1 cup (122g) unsweetened apple sauce
1 tablespoon (16g) peanut butter
1 tablespoon (21g) honey
2 teaspoons (8g) light brown sugar

HOW TO MAKE IT

1. Turn your Rolled Oats into oat flour by processing or blending them until they look like flour
2. Combine all of your dry ingredients into a large bowl aside from your Chocolate Chips and Brown Sugar
3. Mix everything together
4. Take out another bowl and combine all of your wet ingredients into it
5. Mix those together then slowly mix your wet ingredients into your dry ingredients
7. Take out an angel food cake pan, coat it with some non-stick cooking spray, and pour your mix in
8. Evenly distribute your Chocolate Chips and Brown Sugar over the top of your cake
8. Bake on 350F/176C for 20-25 minutes

 $2.20   **25:00**

NUTRITION

Whole Recipe
Makes: 1 Recipe
Calories: 1889
Fat: 49g
Saturated Fat: 18g
Sodium: 887mg
Carbs: 201g
Fiber: 23g
Sugar: 56g
Protein: 161g

1 PIECE
Makes: 10 Pieces
Calories: 188
Fat: 4.9g
Saturated Fat: 1.8g
Sodium: 88.7mg
Carbs: 20.1g
Fiber: 2.3g
Sugar: 5.6g
Protein: 16.1g

15

INGREDIENTS

1 large egg
2 large egg whites
1/2 cup (40g) rolled oats
1 1/2 scoops (45g) chocolate protein powder or vanilla/unflavored
6 tablespoons (45g) coconut flour
5.3 ounces (150g) fat free vanilla greek yogurt or cottage cheese
1/2 cup (4 ounces) coffee
1 teaspoon baking powder

HOW TO MAKE THEM

1. Add all of your ingredients into either a food processor or blender
2. Process or blend everything together until no clumps are left
3. Take out a stove top pan, turn your burner on Medium Heat, and coat your pan with some non-stick cooking spray
4. Pour your mix in and cook each side of your pancake for around 2-3 minutes

 $2.25   **10:00**

COFFEE PANCAKES

NUTRITION

Whole Recipe

Makes: 1 Recipe
Calories: 729
Fat: 17g
Saturated Fat: 8g
Sodium: 544mg
Carbs: 66g
Fiber: 22g
Sugar: 16g
Protein: 78g

FITNESS FRENCH TOAST STICKS

INGREDIENTS

2 large eggs
2 large egg whites
1/2 tablespoon butter
1/2 teaspoon ground cinnamon
1 teaspoon vanilla extract
1 scoop (30g) vanilla protein powder
1/2 cup (4 ounces) unsweetened vanilla almond milk or milk/other milk substitute
4-5 slices of whatever type of bread you want

HOW TO MAKE THEM

1. Melt your Butter
2. Add all of your ingredients (not bread) into either a food processor or blender
3. Process or blend everything together
4. Take out your Bread and cut each piece into 3 pieces
5. Take out and coat a baking sheet with some non-stick cooking spray
6. Dunk each side of your pieces into your mix, let the excess mix drip off, and put them onto your baking sheet
7. Coat the tops of your pieces with some non-stick cooking spray
8. Bake on 350F/176C for 10 minutes
9. After 10 minutes flip your pieces over, coat that side with some non-stick cooking spray, and put them back in the oven for another 10 minutes

TIP

Factor in the calories of your bread once you decide on how many pieces you're eating!

 $2.00   12:00

NUTRITION

In Just The Mix
Makes: 1 Recipe
Calories: 358
Fat: 18g
Saturated Fat: 7g
Sodium: 530mg
Carbs: 3g
Fiber: 1g
Sugar: 3g
Protein: 46g

NUTRITION

Whole Recipe
Makes: 1 Recipe
Calories: 511
Fat: 15g
Saturated Fat: 10g
Sodium: 418mg
Carbs: 48g
Fiber: 9g
Sugar: 19g
Protein: 46g

GREEN ENERGY SMOOTHIE

INGREDIENTS

3/4 cup (6 ounces) unsweetened vanilla almond milk or other milk substitute
1 cup kale or other greens
3/4 cup (6 ounces) green tea
1 banana
1 teaspoon vanilla extract
1 1/2 scoops (60g) vanilla protein powder
1/2 tablespoon (7g) coconut oil
1 cup ice

HOW TO MAKE IT

1. Make your Green Tea
2. Combine all of your ingredients into a blender
3. Blend everything together

 $1.20   5:00

TIP

Don't forget that green tea has caffeine so this smoothie is gonna give you a nice BOOST!

18

LOW CARB BLUEBERRY PANCAKES

INGREDIENTS

2 large eggs or 4 large egg whites
1 teaspoon vanilla extract
2 tablespoons (15g) coconut flour or oat flour
1 scoop (30g) vanilla protein powder
5 ounces (150g) fat free cream cheese
1/2 cup blueberries
1/2 teaspoon baking powder

HOW TO MAKE THEM

1. Combine all of your ingredients aside from 1/4 Cup Blueberries into either a food processor or blender
2. Process or blend everything together
3. Lightly mix in the 1/4 Cup Blueberries you left aside
4. Take out a stove top pan, turn your burner on Medium-High heat, and coat it with some non-stick cooking spray
5. Pour your mix in and cook each side for around 2 minutes

TIPS

Double or triple the recipe to accommodate your appetite!

Make them the night before and reheat them for :30 seconds in the microwave!

 $2.00   **10:00**

NUTRITION

Whole Recipe
Makes: 1 Recipe
Calories: 484
Fat: 16g
Saturated Fat: 7g
Sodium: 502mg
Carbs: 24g
Fiber: 8g
Sugar: 14g
Protein: 61g

MICROWAVE PUMPKIN PANCAKES

INGREDIENTS

1 large egg white
1 ounce unsweetened vanilla almond milk or milk/other milk substitute
1/4 cup (28g) almond flour
1 scoop (30g) vanilla protein powder (optional)
1/2 teaspoon ground cinnamon
1 teaspoon vanilla extract
1/4 cup (61g) pure pumpkin
1/4 teaspoon baking powder
chocolate chips (optional)

NUTRITION

Whole Recipe
Makes: 1 Recipe
Calories: 327
Fat: 15g
Saturated Fat: 1g
Sodium: 244mg
Carbs: 11g
Fiber: 7g
Sugar: 6g
Protein: 37g

HOW TO MAKE THEM

1. Combine all of your ingredients into a bowl aside from your optional Chocolate Chips
2. Mix everything together until the chunks are gone
3. Take out a plate, coat it with some non-stick cooking spray, and pour half of your mix onto it
4. Top your pancakes with some Chocolate Chips or anything else you want
5. Microwave for 1 minute, wait :5 seconds, and microwave for an additional :45 seconds
6. Remove and repeat

 $.70   1:50

MINI BIRTHDAY CAKE MUFFINS

INGREDIENTS

1/2 cup (40g) rolled oats or coconut flour
2 large eggs or 4 large egg whites
2 scoops (60g) vanilla protein powder
1 1/2 tablespoons (31.5g) honey or brown rice syrup
1/4 cup (2 ounces) unsweetened vanilla almond milk or regular milk/other milk substitute
2 teaspoons vanilla extract
16 ounces (454g) reduced sodium chickpeas or other white bean
pinch salt
1 teaspoon baking powder
2 teaspoons rainbow sprinkles

NUTRITION

Whole Recipe
Makes: 1 Recipe
Calories: 1103
Fat: 23g
Saturated Fat: 3g
Sodium: 1088mg
Carbs: 133g
Fiber: 22g
Sugar: 33g
Protein: 91g

1 MUFFIN
Makes: 12 Muffins
Calories: 91
Fat: 1.9g
Saturated Fat: .2g
Sodium: 90.6mg
Carbs: 11g
Fiber: 1.8g
Sugar: 2.7g
Protein: 7.5g

HOW TO MAKE THEM

1. Drain and rinse your Chickpeas
2. Add all of your ingredients into a food processor or really powerful blender aside from your Rainbow Sprinkles
3. Process or blend everything together
4. Lightly mix in your Rainbow Sprinkles
5. Take out a couple muffin pans or some silicone cups, coat them with non-stick cooking spray, and add your mix in leaving 1/4" from the top
6. Bake on 350F/176C for 15-20 minutes

 $1.95   **20:00**

OMELETTE STUFFED BELL PEPPERS

INGREDIENTS

1 bell pepper
1 large egg
2 large egg whites
1 ounce almond milk or milk/other milk substitute
1 tablespoon (7g) bacon bits
1 tablespoon (15g) salsa
1/8 cup (14g) reduced fat cheddar cheese or other cheese
pinch black pepper

NUTRITION

Whole Recipe
Makes: 1 Recipe
Calories: 197
Fat: 9g
Saturated Fat: 4g
Sodium: 332mg
Carbs: 8g
Fiber: 1g
Sugar: 4g
Protein: 21g

HOW TO MAKE THEM

1. Take out a Bell Pepper, cut the top off, and remove the seeds
2. Add the rest of your ingredients into a bowl and mix them together
3. Pour your mix into your Bell Pepper
4. Bake on 350F/176C for 40-45 minutes

 $.75   45:00

TIP

Double or triple the recipe so you can make enough to either satisfy your appetite or feed your family!

ORIGINAL PANCAKES

INGREDIENTS

12 tablespoons (184g) liquid egg whites or 4 large egg whites
1/2 cup (40g) rolled oats
1/2 cup (116g) fat free cottage cheese
1 teaspoon vanilla extract
3 tablespoons (28g) coconut flour
1/2 teaspoon ground cinnamon
1 tablespoon sweetener
1/8 teaspoon salt
1/2 teaspoon baking powder

HOW TO MAKE THEM

1. Combine all of your ingredients into either a food processor or blender
2. Process or blend everything together
3. Take out a stove top pan, turn your burner on Medium Heat, and coat it with some non-stick cooking spray
4. Once your pan heats up, pour your mix in, and cook each side of your pancake for around 2-3 minutes

 $.85   **10:00**

TIP

Add in a scoop of protein powder for even more flavor and protein!

NUTRITION

Whole Recipe

Makes: 1 Recipe
Calories: 438
Fat: 6g
Saturated Fat: 4g
Sodium: 441mg
Carbs: 51g
Fiber: 16g
Sugar: 11g
Protein: 45g

PUMPKIN DOUGHNUTS

INGREDIENTS

1 large egg
3 large egg whites
1/4 cup (61g) pure pumpkin
3 teaspoons (12g) light brown sugar
1 scoop (30g) vanilla protein powder
6 tablespoons (45g) coconut flour
1/2 teaspoon ground cinnamon
1 teaspoon pumpkin pie spice
1/2 tablespoon (7g) coconut oil
1 teaspoon vanilla extract
1 teaspoon baking powder
5.3 ounces (150g) fat free vanilla greek yogurt
halloween sprinkles

NUTRITION

Whole Recipe
Makes: 1 Recipe
Calories: 609
Fat: 21g
Saturated Fat: 20g
Sodium: 479mg
Carbs: 51g
Fiber: 23g
Sugar: 18g
Protein: 54g

1 DOUGHNUT
Makes: 4 Doughnuts
Calories: 152
Fat: 5.2g
Saturated Fat: 5g
Sodium: 119.7mg
Carbs: 12.7g
Fiber: 5.7g
Sugar: 4.5g
Protein: 13.5g

HOW TO MAKE THEM

1. Melt your Coconut Oil
2. Combine all of your ingredients aside from your Greek Yogurt and Halloween Sprinkles into a large bowl
2. Mix those ingredients together
3. Take out a doughnut pan, coat it with some non-stick cooking spray, and pour your mix in
4. Top your doughnuts with whatever you want
5. Bake on 350F/176C for 10-15 minutes
6. Once they cool, top them with some Greek Yogurt and Halloween Sprinkles

 $1.10   15:00

TRIPLE CHOCOLATE DOUGHNUTS

INGREDIENTS

1 large egg
3 large egg whites
6 tablespoons (45g) coconut flour
3 tablespoons (15g) cocoa powder
1 1/2 scoops (45g) chocolate protein powder
1 ounce unsweetened vanilla almond milk or milk/other milk substitute
1 1/2 tablespoons (21g) dark chocolate
1 teaspoon baking powder

NUTRITION

Whole Recipe
Makes: 1 Recipe
Calories: 635
Fat: 23g
Saturated Fat: 12g
Sodium: 612mg
Carbs: 51g
Fiber: 26g
Sugar: 15g
Protein: 56g

1 DOUGHNUT
Makes: 4 Doughnuts
Calories: 158
Fat: 5.7g
Saturated Fat: 3g
Sodium: 153mg
Carbs: 12.7g
Fiber: 6.5g
Sugar: 3.7g
Protein: 14g

HOW TO MAKE THEM

1. Melt your Dark Chocolate
2. Combine all of your ingredients into a bowl
3. Mix everything together
4. Take out a doughnut pan, coat it with some non-stick cooking spray, and pour your mix in
5. Top your doughnuts with whatever you want
6. Bake on 350F/176C for 8-10 minutes

 $1.00   **10:00**

TIP

Glaze them with some protein frosting or Greek yogurt!

25

2 QUICK OATMEAL RECIPES

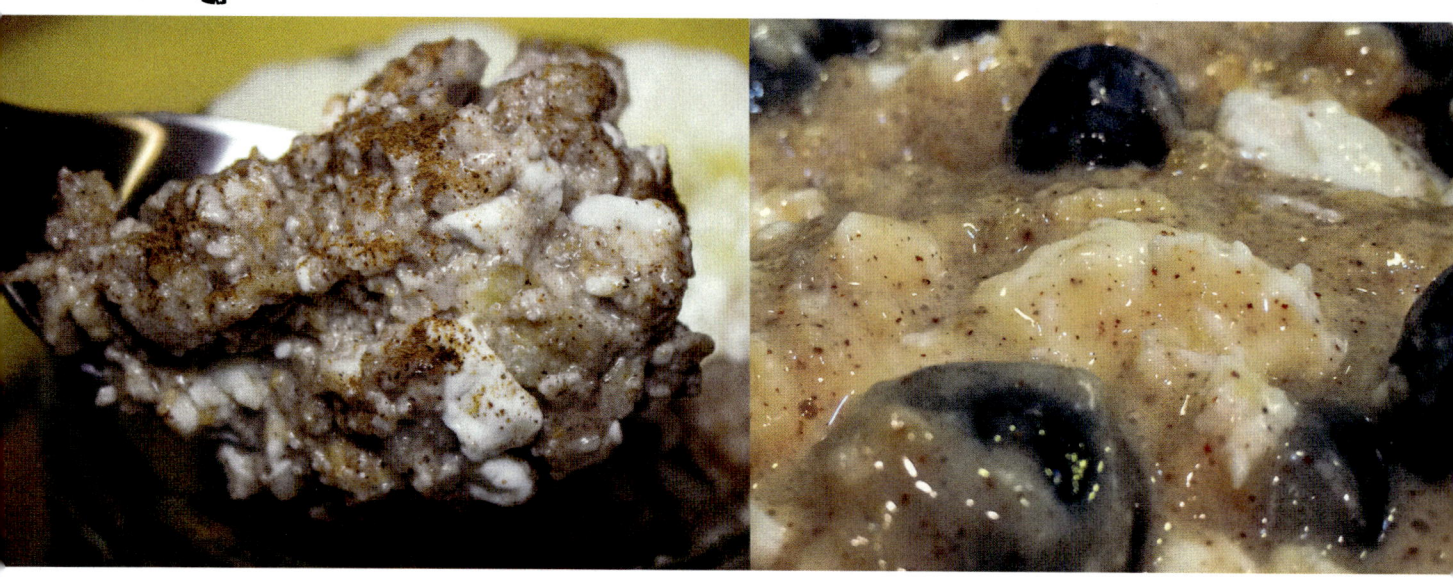

BODYBUILDING OATMEAL

1/2 cup (40g) rolled oats
1/4 cup (2 ounces) unsweetened vanilla almond milk or milk/milk substitute
4 large egg whites
1 1/2 teaspoons vanilla extract
2 tablespoons (32g) peanut butter
1/2 banana
1/2 teaspoon ground cinnamon
1/2 cup (115g) low fat cottage cheese

HOW TO MAKE IT

1. Add your Egg Whites, Almond Milk, and Rolled Oats into a microwavable safe bowl
2. Lightly mix those ingredients together and microwave your oatmeal for 2 minutes or until your Egg Whites look cooked in
3. Add in the rest of your ingredients aside from your Cottage Cheese
4. Mix all of those together while mashing in your Banana
5. Add in your Cottage Cheese and mix that in
6. Add in your Cream Cheese and gently mix that in

 $1.00   2:00

TIP

Add in some honey, brown rice syrup, fresh fruit, or anything else you can think of if it's not sweet enough!

NUTRITION Makes: 1 Recipe

Calories: 589 **Fat: 21g** Saturated Fat: 4g Sodium: 501mg
Carbs: 50g Fiber: 9g Sugar: 12g **Protein: 50g**

CHEESECAKE OATMEAL

1/2 cup (40g) rolled oats
1/2 cup (4 ounces) unsweetened vanilla coconut milk or milk/milk substitute
1/4 cup (2 ounces) water
2 servings (16g) instant sugar free fat free cheesecake pudding
1 scoop (30g) vanilla protein powder
1/2 teaspoon vanilla extract
1/2 teaspoon ground cinnamon
1/2 tablespoon (10.5g) honey
4 tablespoons (60g) fat free cream cheese

HOW TO MAKE IT

1. Take out a microwavable safe bowl and add your Rolled Oats, Milk, Water, and Pudding into it
2. Mix everything together
3. Microwave for around 2 minutes
4. Add in the rest of your ingredients aside from your Cream Cheese
5. Mix those together
6. Add in your Cream Cheese and gently mix that in

 $1.00   2:00

TIP

Put it in the fridge or let it cool down for a bit so it tastes even more like cheesecake!

NUTRITION Makes: 1 Recipe

Calories: 422 **Fat: 6g** Saturated Fat: 3g Sodium: 903mg
Carbs: 56g Fiber: 5g Sugar: 15g **Protein: 36g**

ALL OF THE...
DESSERT RECIPES

BLUEBERRY PIE FLUFF

INGREDIENTS

1 1/2 cups (210g) frozen blueberries
1 scoop (30g) vanilla protein powder
1 teaspoon vanilla extract
1/4 cup (2 ounces) unsweetened vanilla almond milk or milk/other milk substitute
graham cracker

NUTRITION

Whole Recipe
Makes: 1 Recipe
Calories: 270
Fat: 2g
Saturated Fat: 0g
Sodium: 218mg
Carbs: 33g
Fiber: 10g
Sugar: 19g
Protein: 30g

1 BOWL
Makes: 2 Bowls
Calories: 135
Fat: 1g
Saturated Fat: 0g
Sodium: 109mg
Carbs: 16.5g
Fiber: 5g
Sugar: 9.5g
Protein: 15g

HOW TO MAKE IT

1. Add all of your ingredients into a bowl aside from your Graham Cracker
2. Using a hand blender, blend everything together until it's creamy
3. Once it's creamy stop blending, take out a hand mixer or whisk, and mix everything together for 5 minutes or until it's fluffy (it should start to fluff up after around a minute)
4. Top it with a crushed up Graham Cracker

 $.75   **7:00**

TIP

The longer you mix it, the fluffier it'll get!

BROWNIE BATTER DIP

INGREDIENTS

16 ounces (454g) reduced sodium chickpeas
1 teaspoon vanilla extract
1 tablespoon (15g) sugar free chocolate chips
3 scoops (90g) chocolate protein powder
3 ounces unsweetened vanilla almond milk or milk/other milk substitute
3 tablespoons (21g) coconut flour or oat flour
2 tablespoons (37g) nutella
1 serving (11g) instant sugar free fat free chocolate fudge pudding
1 tablespoon sweetener
3 tablespoons (15g) cocoa powder

NUTRITION

Whole Recipe
Makes: 1 Recipe
Calories: 1264
Fat: 32g
Saturated Fat: 10g
Sodium: 1871mg
Carbs: 135g
Fiber: 34g
Sugar: 32g
Protein: 109g

1 BOWL
Makes: 4 Bowls
Calories: 316
Fat: 8g
Saturated Fat: 2.5g
Sodium: 467.7mg
Carbs: 33.7g
Fiber: 8.5g
Sugar: 8g
Protein: 27.2g

HOW TO MAKE IT

1. Combine all of your ingredients into either a blender or food processor
2. Blend or process everything together
3. Pour your mix into a bowl

 $2.40   5:00

TIP

Eat it using some graham crackers!

29

CHOCOLATE CHIP COOKIE DOUGH BROWNIES

INGREDIENTS

1/4 cup (20g) rolled oats
2 large eggs
1 teaspoon vanilla extract
1/4 teaspoon butter extract
2 teaspoons (8g) light brown sugar
2 scoops (60g) vanilla protein powder
16 ounces (454g) reduced sodium chickpeas
1/4 cup (2 ounces) unsweetened vanilla almond milk or milk/other milk substitute
1/4 teaspoons salt
1 teaspoon baking powder
2 tablespoons (30g) semi-sweet chocolate chips

 $1.90   25:00

HOW TO MAKE THEM

1. Combine all of your ingredients aside from your Chocolate Chips into either a food processor or really powerful blender
2. Process or blend everything together
3. Take out a baking pan, coat it with some non-stick cooking spray, and pour your mix in
4. Top them with your Chocolate Chips
5. Bake on 350F/176C for 20-25 minutes

TIPS

If you don't like chocolate chips then top it with some nuts, peanut butter chips, or whatever else you prefer!

Want thicker brownies? Use a smaller pan!

NUTRITION

Whole Recipe
Makes: 1 Recipe
Calories: 1085
Fat: 29g
Saturated Fat: 8g
Sodium: 1288mg
Carbs: 116g
Fiber: 20g
Sugar: 30g
Protein: 90g

1 BROWNIE
Makes: 8 Brownies
Calories: 135
Fat: 3.6g
Saturated Fat: 1g
Sodium: 161mg
Carbs: 14.5g
Fiber: 2.5g
Sugar: 3.7g
Protein: 11.2g

CHOCOLATE OR VANILLA CUPCAKES

INGREDIENTS

cupcakes
2 cups (160g) rolled oats
1/2 cup (56g) almond flour
1 tablespoon apple cider vinegar
1 cup (244g) unsweetened apple sauce
3 scoops (90g) vanilla protein powder
1 teaspoon vanilla extract
2 tablespoons (44g) brown rice syrup or honey
4 large egg whites
1/4 teaspoon salt
1 1/2 teaspoons baking powder
1/4 cup (2 ounces) unsweetened vanilla almond milk or milk/other milk substitute
4 tablespoons (20g) cocoa powder (optional)

frosting
5.3 ounces (150g) fat free vanilla Greek yogurt
1 scoop (30g) vanilla protein powder
1 teaspoon vanilla extract

HOW TO MAKE THEM

1. Combine all of your ingredients into a food processor or blender
2. Process or blend everything together
3. Take out a muffin pan and coat it with some non-stick cooking spray or silicone cups
4. Bake on 350F/176C for 15-20 minutes
5. Once they cool combine all of your frosting ingredients together, mix, and top them with your frosting!

 $2.00   **20:00**

TIP

Make them chocolate by using chocolate protein powder or by adding in the optional cocoa powder!

NUTRITION

Whole Recipe
Makes: 1 Recipe
Calories: 1333
Fat: 37g
Saturated Fat: 3g
Sodium: 821mg
Carbs: 135g
Fiber: 18g
Sugar: 49g
Protein: 115g

1 CUPCAKE
Makes: 14 Cupcakes
Calories: 95
Fat: 2.6g
Saturated Fat: .2g
Sodium: 58.6mg
Carbs: 9.6g
Fiber: 1.2g
Sugar: 3.5g
Protein: 8.2g

COOKIES & CREAM MUG CAKE

INGREDIENTS

6 tablespoons (92g) liquid egg whites or 2 large egg whites
3 tablespoons (28g) coconut flour or oat flour
1/2 tablespoon (7.5g) semi-sweet chocolate chips
1 teaspoon vanilla extract
2.65 ounces (75g) fat free vanilla greek yogurt
4 1/2 mini cookies (14.5g)
1 tablespoon (6g) marshmallow fluff
1 scoop (30g) vanilla protein powder
1/2 teaspoon baking powder

NUTRITION

Whole Recipe
Makes: 1 Recipe
Calories: 440
Fat: 8g
Saturated Fat: 4g
Sodium: 344mg
Carbs: 43g
Fiber: 13g
Sugar: 18g
Protein: 49g

HOW TO MAKE IT

1. Crush up your Mini Cookies, add all of your ingredients into a bowl, and mix everything together
2. Take out a mug and coat it with some non-stick cooking spray
3. Add your mix into it
4. Microwave your mug for :30 seconds
5. Quickly mix everything together again
6. Microwave for an additional :90 seconds

 $1.00   2:00

TIP

Make your mix the night before so it's ready to go whenever you want to make it!

HEALTHY BIRTHDAY CAKE

INGREDIENTS

2 cups (160g) rolled oats
8 tablespoons (56g) coconut flour
1/4 cup sweetener
1/2 teaspoon salt
3 teaspoons baking powder
3 scoops (90g) vanilla protein powder
3 large egg whites
1 1/2 tablespoons (21g) coconut oil
1 tablespoon (21g) honey or brown rice syrup
5.3 ounces (150g) fat free plain greek yogurt
1/2 cup (4 ounces) sugar free vanilla coconut milk or milk/milk substitute
1 teaspoon vanilla extract
2 tablespoons (30g) sugar free chocolate chips

HOW TO MAKE IT

1. Turn your Rolled Oats into oat flour by processing or blending them until they look like flour
2. Combine all of your dry ingredients into a large bowl aside from your Chocolate Chips
3. Mix everything together
4. Take out another bowl and combine all of your wet ingredients into it
5. Mix those together then slowly mix your wet ingredients into your dry ingredients
7. Lightly mix in your Chocolate Chips
8. Take out a baking pan or dish, coat it with some non-stick cooking spray, and pour your mix in
9. Bake on 350F/176C for 20-25 minutes

 $3.00   **30:00**

TIP

Top it using some protein frosting!

NUTRITION

Whole Recipe
Makes: 1 Recipe
Calories: 1913
Fat: 45g
Saturated Fat: 32g
Sodium: 1794mg
Carbs: 194g
Fiber: 37g
Sugar: 58g
Protein: 183g

1 PIECE
Makes: 8 Pieces
Calories: 239
Fat: 5.6g
Saturated Fat: 4g
Sodium: 224.2mg
Carbs: 24.2g
Fiber: 4.6g
Sugar: 7.2g
Protein: 22.8g

LOW FAT PEANUT BUTTER

INGREDIENTS

3 scoops (90g) vanilla protein powder
16 ounces (454g) reduced sodium chickpeas or other white bean
8 tablespoons (48g) powdered peanut butter or peanut flour
2 tablespoons (18g) coconut flour
1/4 cup (2 ounces) unsweetened vanilla almond milk or milk/other milk substitute
1 tablespoon peanut oil

NUTRITION

Whole Recipe
Makes: 1 Recipe
Calories: 1208
Fat: 32g
Saturated Fat: 4g
Sodium: 1102mg
Carbs: 107g
Fiber: 34g
Sugar: 16g
Protein: 123g

1 BOWL
Makes: 10 Bowls
Calories: 120
Fat: 3.2g
Saturated Fat: .4g
Sodium: 110.2mg
Carbs: 10.7g
Fiber: 3.4g
Sugar: 1.6g
Protein: 12.3g

HOW TO MAKE IT

1. Drain and rinse your Chickpeas
2. Add all of your ingredients into either a really powerful blender or food processor
3. Blend or process everything together until it looks like peanut butter

 $1.95   5:00

TIP

Store your recipe in the fridge and it'll usually last around 7-10 days!

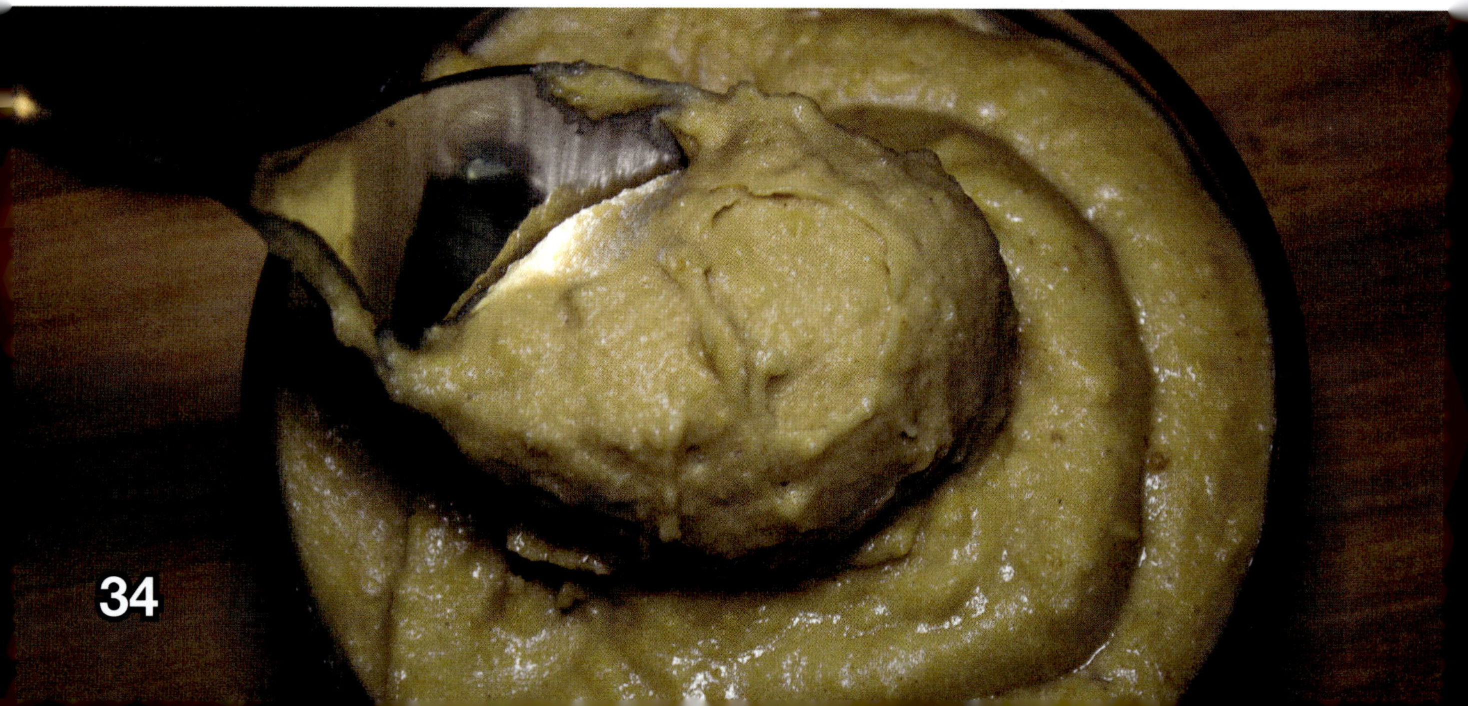

M&M CAKE JARS

NUTRITION

Whole Recipe
Makes: 1 Recipe
Calories: 654
Fat: 26g
Saturated Fat: 10g
Sodium: 470mg
Carbs: 55g
Fiber: 22g
Sugar: 23g
Protein: 50g

1 JAR
Makes: 2 Jars
Calories: 327
Fat: 13g
Saturated Fat: 5g
Sodium: 235mg
Carbs: 27.5g
Fiber: 11g
Sugar: 11.5g
Protein: 25g

INGREDIENTS

1 large egg
1 large egg white
1 scoop (30g) vanilla protein powder
1/2 cup (4 ounces) unsweetened vanilla almond milk or milk/other milk substitute
1 teaspoon vanilla extract
6 tablespoons (45g) coconut flour
1/8 cup (14g) almond flour
1/2 banana
1/2 teaspoon baking powder
1 tablespoon (14g) mini baking m&m's

HOW TO MAKE THEM

1. Add all of your ingredients into a bowl aside from your M&M's
2. Mix everything around until it's smooth
3. Lightly mix in your M&M's
4. Take out two half pint size (or bigger) mason jars, coat them with some non-stick cooking spray, and evenly distribute your mix into them
5. Top them with some M&M's or whatever else you want
6. Put them in the oven on 350F/176C for 25-30 minutes

TIP

Not enough protein? Give it more flavor AND protein by adding some protein frosting on top once it cools!

$1.50   30:00

MOLTEN LAVA CAKES

INGREDIENTS

3 ounces sugar free vanilla coconut milk or milk/other milk substitute
1 teaspoon vanilla extract
1/2 cup (40g) rolled oats
1 tablespoon sweetener
1/2 tablespoon (7g) coconut oil
2 tablespoons (10g) cocoa powder
1 scoop (30g) chocolate protein powder
1 teaspoon instant coffee
1/4 cup (61g) unsweetened apple sauce
1/2 teaspoon salt
1 teaspoon baking powder
1/2 tablespoon (7.5g) sugar free chocolate chips (per cake)
1 tablespoon (17g) sugar free strawberry jelly (per cake)

HOW TO MAKE THEM

1. Turn your Rolled Oats into oat flour by processing or blending them until they look like flour
2. Add all of your ingredients aside from your Chocolate Chips and Jelly into a bowl
3. Mix everything together
4. Take out 2 1 cup ramekins and coat them with some non-stick cooking spray
5. Fill each ramekin up about halfway
6. Add 1/2 Tablespoon of Chocolate Chips and 1 Tablespoon of Jelly to the center of each one
7. Evenly distribute the rest of your mix into each ramekin
8. Bake on 350F/176C for 13-16 minutes

$1.60   16:00

NUTRITION

Whole Recipe
Makes: 1 Recipe
Calories: 542
Fat: 18g
Saturated Fat: 11g
Sodium: 289mg
Carbs: 61g
Fiber: 16g
Sugar: 8g
Protein: 34g

1 CAKE
Makes: 2 Cakes
Calories: 271
Fat: 9g
Saturated Fat: 5.5g
Sodium: 144.5mg
Carbs: 30.5g
Fiber: 8g
Sugar: 4g
Protein: 17g

NO BAKE NUTELLA BARS

INGREDIENTS

1/2 cup (4 ounces) unsweetened vanilla almond milk or milk/other milk substitute
6 tablespoons (45g) coconut flour
1/2 cup (40g) rolled oats
3 Scoops (90g) chocolate protein powder
1 tablespoon (5g) cocoa powder
1 tablespoon (18.5g) nutella
3 tablespoons (45g) dark chocolate chips

HOW TO MAKE THEM

1. Combine all of your ingredients aside from your Chocolate Chips into a food processor or really powerful blender
2. Process or blend everything together until it starts to get clumpy
3. Shape your mix into bars
4. Take out a stove top pan, turn your burner on Low Heat, and add your Chocolate Chips into it
5. Slowly melt your Chocolate Chips while occasionally stirring them so they don't burn
6. Top your bars with your melted chocolate and put them in the fridge for 20 minutes or until the chocolate hardens around them

$1.20   20:00

NUTRITION

Whole Recipe
Makes: 1 Recipe
Calories: 1108
Fat: 36g
Saturated Fat: 18g
Sodium: 700mg
Carbs: 98g
Fiber: 28g
Sugar: 35g
Protein: 98g

1 BAR
Makes: 3 Bars
Calories: 369
Fat: 12g
Saturated Fat: 6g
Sodium: 233.3mg
Carbs: 32.6g
Fiber: 9.3g
Sugar: 11.6g
Protein: 32.6g

37

ORANGE CREAM ANYTHING

INGREDIENTS

2 large eggs
1 teaspoon vanilla extract
2 slices orange zest
1/2 orange
2 tablespoons (28g) olive oil
1 tablespoon (14g) coconut oil
1 cup (120g) whole wheat pastry flour
1 1/2 scoops (45g) vanilla protein powder
1/4 cup sweetener
1 teaspoon baking powder
1/2 teaspoon baking soda
1/2 teaspoon salt

HOW TO MAKE IT/THEM

1. Shave 2 slices of Zest off your Orange
2. Peel your Orange
3. Add all of your ingredients into a food processor and process them together
4. Take out a either a bread, cake, or cupcake pan and coat it with some non-stick cooking spray
5. Evenly distribute your mix into your pan
6. Bake on 350F/176C for 15 minutes

TIP

Top whatever you make with some protein frosting and orange slices!

NUTRITION

Whole Recipe
Makes: 1 Recipe
Calories: 1449
Fat: 57g
Saturated Fat: 22g
Sodium: 904mg
Carbs: 118g
Fiber: 20g
Sugar: 19g
Protein: 116g

1 SQUARE
Makes: 10 Squares
Calories: 724
Fat: 28.5g
Saturated Fat: 11g
Sodium: 452mg
Carbs: 59g
Fiber: 10g
Sugar: 9.5g
Protein: 58g

$3.40   15:00

INGREDIENTS

12 ounces (339g) fat free cream cheese
12 ounces (340g) fat free vanilla greek yogurt
2 large egg
1 teaspoon vanilla extract
1/4 cup (2 ounces) fat free milk or milk substitute
2 scoops (60g) vanilla protein powder
1 teaspoon lemon juice

TIP

Change the flavor of your cheesecake up by using different flavor Greek yogurt and protein powder or by adding in things like cookies, sprinkles extracts, fruits, nuts and so on!

HOW TO MAKE IT

1. Take out a large bowl, add all of your ingredients into it, and mix everything together
2. Line a 6x2 cake pan with some parchment paper and pour your mix in
3. Bake on 325F/162C for 30-35 minutes
4. After 30-35 minutes drop your temperature to 200F/93C for another 50-60 minutes
5. Take your cheesecake out, let it cool, wrap it up, and put it into the fridge overnight (or a couple hours if you can't wait that long)
6. Top it with some Greek yogurt or protein frosting and whatever else you want

$4.00   95:00

ORIGINAL PROTEIN CHEESECAKE

NUTRITION

Whole Recipe
Makes: 1 Recipe
Calories: 787
Fat: 11g
Saturated Fat: 4g
Sodium: 2745mg
Carbs: 37g
Fiber: 0g
Sugar: 28g
Protein: 135g

1 PIECE
Makes: 4 Pieces
Calories: 196
Fat: 2.7g
Saturated Fat: 1g
Sodium: 686.2mg
Carbs: 9.2g
Fiber: 0g
Sugar: 7g
Protein: 33.7g

PEANUT BUTTER CUPS

INGREDIENTS

2 tablespoons (32g) peanut butter
2 tablespoons (12g) powdered peanut butter or peanut flour
1 teaspoon vanilla extract
1 scoop (30g) vanilla protein powder
1/4 cup (61g) reduced sodium chickpeas or other white bean
1/2 ounce unsweetened vanilla almond milk or milk/other milk substitute
2 tablespoons (28g) dark chocolate

HOW TO MAKE THEM

1. Combine all of your ingredients aside from your Dark Chocolate into a food processor or really powerful blender
2. Process or blend everything together until it starts to clump up (be careful not to burn out your motor)
3. Take out a muffin pan or silicone cups and evenly distribute your mix into however many you want to make
4. Melt your Dark Chocolate
5. Evenly distribute your melted chocolate on top
6. Put them in the freezer for 10-15 minutes so that they can harden up

TIP

Add some melted chocolate into the bottom of your pan or cups to completely coat them!

$1.10   15:00

NUTRITION

Whole Recipe
Makes: 1 Recipe
Calories: 563
Fat: 27g
Saturated Fat: 8g
Sodium: 455mg
Carbs: 37g
Fiber: 9g
Sugar: 17g
Protein: 43g

1 CUP
Makes: 4 Cups
Calories: 140
Fat: 6.7g
Saturated Fat: 2g
Sodium: 113.7mg
Carbs: 9.2g
Fiber: 2.2g
Sugar: 4.2g
Protein: 10.7g

PEANUT BUTTER SQUARES

INGREDIENTS

16 ounces (454g) reduced sodium chickpeas or other white bean
6 tablespoons (96g) peanut butter
2 teaspoons vanilla extract
2 tablespoons (44g) brown rice syrup or honey
4 scoops (120g) vanilla protein powder
1 teaspoon baking powder
1 1/2 tablespoons (22.5g) dark chocolate chips

HOW TO MAKE THEM

1. Drain and rinse your Chickpeas
2. Add all of your ingredients aside from your Chocolate Chips into either a food processor or really powerful blender
3. Process or blend everything together
4. Take out a baking pan, coat it with some non-stick cooking spray, and pour your mix in
5. Top your squares with your Chocolate Chips
6. Put them in the oven on 350F/176C for 20-25 minutes

$1.50   25:00

TIP

Check to see if they're done by inserting a toothpick into the center of your squares and if it comes out clean, they're done!

NUTRITION

Whole Recipe
Makes: 1 Recipe
Calories: 1764
Fat: 72g
Saturated Fat: 14g
Sodium: 1570mg
Carbs: 157g
Fiber: 37g
Sugar: 43g
Protein: 122g

1 SQUARE
Makes: 10 Squares
Calories: 176
Fat: 7.2g
Saturated Fat: 1.4g
Sodium: 157mg
Carbs: 15.7g
Fiber: 3.7g
Sugar: 4.3g
Protein: 12.2g

PROTEIN FROSTING I, II & III

HOW TO MAKE THEM

1. Combine all of your ingredients together into a bowl
2. Mix everything together
3. Put them in the fridge if you want them to thicken up even more

💲 $.80-$1.20 ⏱ 2:00

TIPS

Let your cream cheese soften up before mixing it to make it easier!

Add in cocoa powder, melted chocolate chips, peanut butter, marshmallow, caramel, cake mixes or anything else you can think of to switch up the flavor even more!

FROSTING I

4 ounces (120g) fat free cream cheese
1 teaspoon vanilla extract
1 scoop (30g) vanilla protein powder
6 tablespoons (27g) whipped topping

FROSTING II

1 scoop (30g) chocolate protein powder
1 serving (11g) instant sugar free fat free chocolate pudding
1 ounce unsweetened vanilla almond milk or milk/other milk substitute

FROSTING III

5.3 ounces (150g) fat free vanilla greek yogurt
1 scoop (30g) vanilla protein powder
1/4 cup (61g) fat free cottage cheese
food coloring *optional (use it sparringly to change the color of your frosting)

NUTRITION

FROSTING I
Makes: **1 Recipe**
Calories: 281
Fat: 1g
Saturated Fat: 0g
Sodium: 418mg
Carbs: 26g
Fiber: 0g
Sugar: 16g
Protein: 42g

FROSTING II
Makes: **1 Recipe**
Calories: 153
Fat: 1g
Saturated Fat: 0g
Sodium: 372mg
Carbs: 10g
Fiber: 0g
Sugar: 3g
Protein: 26g

FROSTING III
Makes: **1 Recipe**
Calories: 245
Fat: 1g
Saturated Fat: 0g
Sodium: 326mg
Carbs: 14g
Fiber: 0g
Sugar: 12g
Protein: 45g

PUMPKIN PIE CUPCAKES

INGREDIENTS

15 ounces (425g) pure pumpkin
2 large eggs
1/4 cup (2 ounces) unsweetened vanilla almond milk or milk/other milk substitute
6 tablespoons (42g) coconut flour
2 scoops (60g) vanilla protein powder
1 teaspoon vanilla extract
1/2 teaspoon ground cinnamon
1 1/2 teaspoons pumpkin pie spice
2 teaspoons (8g) light brown sugar
4 1/2 tablespoons (27g) graham cracker crumbs
5.3 ounces (150g) pumpkin or vanilla greek yogurt
1/3 cup sweetener
1/4 teaspoon salt
1/2 teaspoon baking powder

HOW TO MAKE THEM

1. Combine all of your ingredients into a food processor or blender aside from 3 Tablespoons (18g) Graham Cracker Crumbs
2. Process or blend everything together
3. Take out 12 silicone cups or a cupcake pan and coat them/it with some non-stick cooking spray
4. Evenly distribute your mix into your silicone cups or pan
5. Top your cupcakes with the 3 Tablespoons (18g) Graham Cracker Crumbs you left aside
6. Bake on 350F/176C for 25-30 minutes

$2.50 **30:00**

TIP

Top your cupcakes with either some Greek yogurt, protein frosting, or whipped cream!

NUTRITION

Whole Recipe
Makes: 1 Recipe
Calories: 1002
Fat: 26g
Saturated Fat: 11g
Sodium: 861mg
Carbs: 105g
Fiber: 27g
Sugar: 48g
Protein: 87g

1 CUPCAKE
Makes: 12 Cupcakes
Calories: 83
Fat: 2.1g
Saturated Fat: .9g
Sodium: 71.7mg
Carbs: 8.7g
Fiber: 2.2g
Sugar: 4g
Protein: 7.2g

S'MORES COOKIE DOUGH

INGREDIENTS

3 ounces unsweetened vanilla almond milk or milk/other milk substitute
1 tablespoon (21g) honey
3 tablespoons (21g) coconut flour or oat flour
3 tablespoons (48g) peanut butter or other nut butter
16 ounces (454g) reduced sodium chickpeas or other white bean
3 scoops (90g) vanilla protein powder
2 teaspoons vanilla extract
1/2 teaspoon butter extract
3 tablespoons sweetener
2 low fat graham crackers
4 tablespoons (10g) marshmallow bits
1 tablespoon (15g) sugar free chocolate chips

HOW TO MAKE IT

1. Combine all of your ingredients aside from your Graham Crackers, Marshmallows Bits, and Chocolate Chips into either a blender or food processor
2. Blend or process everything together
3. Pour your mix into a bowl
4. Top it with your Graham Crackers that you're going to crush up, Marshmallow Bits, and Chocolate Chips

$2.50   5:00

TIP

Bake on 350F/176C for 5-10 minutes if you want to eat it hot!

NUTRITION

Whole Recipe
Makes: 1 Recipe
Calories: 1411
Fat: 43g
Saturated Fat: 11g
Sodium: 1295mg
Carbs: 141g
Fiber: 30g
Sugar: 40g
Protein: 115g

1 BOWL
Makes: 4 Bowls
Calories: 352
Fat: 10.7g
Saturated Fat: 2.7g
Sodium: 323.7mg
Carbs: 35.2g
Fiber: 7.5g
Sugar: 10g
Protein: 28.7g

THE BEST HOMEMADE BARS

INGREDIENTS

14 tablespoons (224g) peanut butter
5 ounces unsweetened vanilla almond milk or milk/other milk substitute
2 tablespoons (44g) brown rice syrup or honey
1 3/4 cups (140g) rolled oats
2 teaspoon vanilla extract
2 teaspoons ground cinnamon
4 1/2 scoops (135g) vanilla protein powder

HOW TO MAKE IT

1. Take out a stove top pan and turn your burner on Low Heat
2. Combine your Peanut Butter, Milk, and Brown Rice Syrup into it
3. Stir those ingredients around on Low Heat for a couple minutes or until everything is mixed together
4. Add in the rest of your ingredients
5. Mix everything together for another couples minutes while on Low Heat
6. Take out a pan or dish, line it with some parchment paper, add your mix in, and shape your bars
7. Press whatever you want into the top of them
8. Put them in the fridge until they harden up (around 1-2 hours)
9. Cut them

TIPS

Add in more milk if your mix appears too dry!

Top them with some dried fruit, nuts, sprinkles, chips, chunks, candy, or anything else you want!

$1.50   10:00

NUTRITION

Whole Recipe
Makes: 1 Recipe
Calories: 2553
Fat: 121g
Saturated Fat: 26g
Sodium: 1504mg
Carbs: 182g
Fiber: 31g
Sugar: 59g
Protein: 184g

1 BAR
Makes: 10 Bars
Calories: 255
Fat: 12.1g
Saturated Fat: 2.6g
Sodium: 150.4mg
Carbs: 18.2g
Fiber: 3.1g
Sugar: 5.9g
Protein: 18.4g

THE BEST PROTEIN COOKIES

INGREDIENTS

1 1/2 cups (120g) rolled oats
1 teaspoon baking powder
2 1/2 scoops (75g) vanilla protein powder
1/4 teaspoon salt
1 teaspoon ground cinnamon
1 large egg
2 teaspoons vanilla extract
10 teaspoons (40g) light brown sugar
1/2 cup (122g) unsweetened apple sauce or 1 banana
4 tablespoons (56g) coconut oil

NUTRITION

Whole Recipe
Makes: 1 Recipe
Calories: 1639
Fat: 71g
Saturated Fat: 57g
Sodium: 827mg
Carbs: 141g
Fiber: 17g
Sugar: 65g
Protein: 109g

1 COOKIE
Makes: 10 Cookies
Calories: 163
Fat: 7.1g
Saturated Fat: 5.7g
Sodium: 82.7mg
Carbs: 14.1g
Fiber: 1.7g
Sugar: 6.5g
Protein: 10.9g

$ $2.50   ⏱ 15:00

HOW TO MAKE THEM

1. Turn your Rolled Oats into oat flour by blending or processing them until they look like flour
2. Add your Oat Flour, Baking Powder, Protein Powder, Salt, and Ground Cinnamon into a bowl
3. Mix those together
4. Melt your Coconut Oil
5. Combine your Egg, Vanilla Extract, Brown Sugar, Apple Sauce, and melted Coconut Oil into a bowl
6. Mix those together
7. Slowly add your dry ingredients into your wet ingredients while mixing everything together
8. Lightly mix in sprinkles, chunks, chips, or anything else you want
9. Cover and put your dough in the fridge for around 1-2 hours or until it hardens up
10. Take out a baking pan and line it with parchment paper
11. Shape your mix into balls and put them onto your baking pan
12. Bake them for 8-10 minutes on 350F/176C

2 QUICK PROTEIN SHAKES

POST-WORKOUT MILKSHAKE

1 1/2 cups (12 ounces) unsweetened vanilla almond milk or milk/other milk substitute
1 scoop (30g) chocolate protein powder
3 tablespoons (15g) cocoa powder
1/2 cup (40g) rolled oats
1 teaspoon vanilla extract
1/2 cup (113g) fat free cottage cheese
1 tablespoon (15g) dark chocolate chips

HOW TO MAKE IT

1. Melt your Chocolate Chips
2. Combine all of your ingredients into a blender
3. Blend everything together

$1.00   2:00

Whole Shake
Makes: 1 Recipe
Calories: 577
Fat: 21g
Saturated Fat: 5g
Sodium: 743mg
Carbs: 13g
Fiber: 2g
Sugar: 7g
Protein: 84g

TIP

Add in some nut butter for some extract fats!

STRAWBERRY BANANA

1 cup (8 ounces) unsweetened vanilla almond milk or milk/other milk substitute
1/2 banana
1 cup strawberries
9 tablespoons (138g) liquid egg whites
5.3 ounces (150g) fat free vanilla greek yogurt
1 teaspoon vanilla extract
1/2 cup ice

HOW TO MAKE IT

1. Combine all of your ingredients into a blender
2. Blend everything together

$1.00   2:00

Whole Shake
Makes: 1 Recipe
Calories: 331
Fat: 7g
Saturated Fat: 1g
Sodium: 393mg
Carbs: 34g
Fiber: 5g
Sugar: 20g
Protein: 33g

TIP

Add in a scoop of protein powder for even more protein!

:60 SECOND NO BAKE CHEESECAKE

INGREDIENTS

6 tablespoons (90g) fat free cream cheese
2 tablespoons fat free vanilla greek yogurt
1 teaspoon vanilla extract
1/2 teaspoon lemon juice
1/4 teaspoon butter extract or 1/2 tablespoon butter
2 teaspoons sweetener
1 scoop (30g) vanilla protein powder

TIPS

Change the flavor of your cheesecake up by using different flavor Greek yogurt and protein powder or by adding in things like cookies, sprinkles extracts, fruits, nuts and so on.

Want it chocolate? Use a couple tablespoons of cocoa powder, a couple melted chocolate chips, and chocolate protein powder!

HOW TO MAKE IT

1. Take out a bowl and add all of your ingredients into it
2. Mix those ingredients together
3. Pour your mix into a smaller bowl(s)
4. For more of a cheesecake like texture, wrap it up and put it into the fridge for a couple hours

$1.10   1:00

ADD A CRUST

Add a quick crust by crushing up a graham cracker into the bottom of your bowl(s)!

NUTRITION

Whole Recipe
Makes: 1 Recipe
Calories: 279
Fat: 0g
Saturated Fat: 0g
Sodium: 392mg
Carbs: 22g
Fiber: 0g
Sugar: 15g
Protein: 41g

ALL OF THE...
LUNCH & DINNER

BAKED LEAN PESTO

INGREDIENTS

3 pounds (48 ounces) chicken breast or any other lean thicker cut protein
1/2 cup (124g) basil pesto
1/2 cup (126g) marinara
2 sliced plum tomatoes
6 tablespoons (30g) grated parmesan cheese
1/2 cup (56g) reduced fat mozzarella cheese

HOW TO MAKE IT

1. Trim the fat off your Chicken Breast or other lean protein, and cut them in half the long way
2. Take out a baking dish and add your chicken into it
3. Evenly distribute your Pesto, Marinara, and Tomatoes on top
4. Cover your dish with aluminum foil and bake on 375F/190C for 25 minutes
5. Take your chicken out and uncover it
6. Top it with your Parmesan and Mozzarella Cheese
7. Bake uncovered for another 10 minutes on 375F/190C

💰 $7.75   ⏱ 35:00

TIPS

Reheat your chicken in the microwave by cutting a slit down the center of your chicken and microwaving it for around 1 minute!

This recipe will last around 5-7 days in the fridge!

Turkey breast is a fantastic substitute for chicken in this recipe!

NUTRITION

Whole Recipe
Makes: 1 Recipe
Calories: 2154
Fat: 90g
Saturated Fat: 19g
Sodium: 1420mg
Carbs: 26g
Fiber: 3g
Sugar: 17g
Protein: 310g

1 PLATE
Makes: 6 Plates
Calories: 359
Fat: 15g
Saturated Fat: 3.1g
Sodium: 236.6mg
Carbs: 4.3g
Fiber: .5g
Sugar: 2.8g
Protein: 51.6g

BAKED CRUSTED FISH

INGREDIENTS

1/2 tablespoon olive oil
1 pound (16 ounces) fish of your choice
lemon juice
6 tablespoons (30g) grated parmesan cheese
3/4 teaspoon garlic powder
1/4 teaspoon black pepper
2 tablespoons (13g) flax seed
2/3 cup (60g) seasoned bread crumbs (or crushed up crackers)
3 1/2 tablespoons butter or butter substitute

HOW TO MAKE IT

1. Take out a baking dish and pour your Olive Oil into it
2. Place your Fish into your baking dish
3. Squirt some Lemon Juice on the top of each piece
4. Take out a bowl and mix together everything but your Butter
5. Evenly distribute your mix on top of each piece
6. Melt your Butter
7. Slowly pour your Butter over each piece (attempt to cover all of your mix)
8. Bake on 450F/232C for 8-12 minutes

TIP

Coat the top of your fish with some non-stick cooking spray if you can't manage to top all of your mix with the butter (this will give it a nice crust)!

NUTRITION

Whole Recipe
Makes: 1 Recipe
Calories: 1020
Fat: 48g
Saturated Fat: 16g
Sodium: 906mg
Carbs: 44g
Fiber: 10g
Sugar: 4g
Protein: 103g

1 PLATE
Makes: 4 Plates
Calories: 255
Fat: 12g
Saturated Fat: 4g
Sodium: 226.5mg
Carbs: 11g
Fiber: 2.5g
Sugar: 1g
Protein: 25.7g

$4.70   12:00

BODYBUILDING GRILLED CHEESE

NUTRITION

Whole Recipe
Makes: 1 Recipe
Calories: 454
Fat: 18g
Saturated Fat: 3g
Sodium: 985mg
Carbs: 33g
Fiber: 5g
Sugar: 6g
Protein: 40g

INGREDIENTS

2 pieces bread
2 slices fat free sharp cheddar cheese
1 slice fat free american cheese
2 pieces turkey bacon
1 tablespoon (14g) sundried tomato & basil hummus (1/2 tablespoon/7g on each piece of bread)
2 large egg whites
1 large egg
1/2 tablespoon olive oil (1/4 tablespoon on each piece of bread)

HOW TO MAKE IT

1. Separately cook your Bacon, Egg, and Egg Whites
2. Take out your Bread and start by spreading 1/2 your Hummus on each piece, 2 slices Cheddar Cheese on one piece, 1 slice American Cheese on the other, evenly divide up your Bacon, and last your cooked Egg and Egg Whites on one piece
3. Close off your sandwich and spread 1/2 your Olive Oil on both the top and bottom
4. Take out a stove top pan or griddle, turn your burner on Medium Heat, and coat it with some non-stick cooking spray
5. Once your pan or griddle heats up coat the side of your sandwich that's going down onto the pan with some non-stick cooking spray and cook that side while pressing down until your cheese is melted
6. Coat the other side with some non-stick cooking spray and repeat until your cheese is melted
7. Once both sides of cheese are melted, your sandwich is done

$1.25   10:00

BODYBUILDING MAC & CHEESE

INGREDIENTS

6 ounces (168g) pasta
2 cans chicken or tuna
3/4 cup (84g) reduced fat sharp cheddar cheese
3 tablespoons (15g) parmesan & romano grated cheese
1 teaspoon garlic powder
1/4 teaspoon onion salt
5.3 ounces (150g) fat free plain greek yogurt

NUTRITION

Whole Recipe
Makes: 1 Recipe
Calories: 1227
Fat: 31g
Saturated Fat: 12g
Sodium: 1780mg
Carbs: 125g
Fiber: 12g
Sugar: 13g
Protein: 112g

1 BOWL
Makes: 4 Bowls
Calories: 306
Fat: 7.7g
Saturated Fat: 3g
Sodium: 445mg
Carbs: 31.2g
Fiber: 3g
Sugar: 3.2g
Protein: 28g

HOW TO MAKE IT

1. Take out a large bowl, drain your Chicken or Tuna, and add it into the bowl
2. Take out whatever you use to boil pasta, add your Pasta into it, and cook it for however long your box says to
3. Turn your burner off, drain it, and put your pasta back into whatever you used
4. Add in your Cheeses and mix them around until they're melted
5. Add in your Garlic Powder, Onion Salt, and Greek Yogurt
6. Mix those in
7. Add in your Chicken or Tuna and mix that in

$3.25   15:00

53

BURRITO PIE

NUTRITION

Whole Recipe
Makes: 1 Recipe
Calories: 1815
Fat: 59g
Saturated Fat: 22g
Sodium: 2109mg
Carbs: 141g
Fiber: 23g
Sugar: 30g
Protein: 180g

1 PIECE
Makes: 8 Piece
Calories: 226
Fat: 7.3g
Saturated Fat: 2.7g
Sodium: 263.6mg
Carbs: 17.6g
Fiber: 2.8g
Sugar: 3.7g
Protein: 22.5g

INGREDIENTS

1 1/2 pounds (24 ounces) lean ground beef or turkey
1/2 cup red onion
4 tablespoons (32g) sliced olives
4 tablespoons (60g) diced green chiles
1 cup (252g) no salt added diced tomatoes
16 tablespoons (244g) salsa
2 whole wheat tortillas
1 cup (244g) reduced sodium black beans or other beans
1 cup (112g) reduced fat mexican style cheese or other cheese

HOW TO MAKE IT

1. Chop up your Red Onion, take out a large stove top pan, turn your burn on Medium-High, and let it heat up
2. Once it heats up add in your Lean Ground Beef or Turkey and brown it
3. After you've browned it add in your Red Onion, Olives, Green Chiles, Diced Tomatoes, and 1/2 of your Salsa
4. Mix everything around, turn your burner on Low Heat, and let it simmer for 15 minutes
5. Take out at least a 9" round baking dish, coat it with some non-stick cooking spray, and add 1 Tortilla on the bottom of it
6. On top of your tortilla put half of your mix, 1/2 your Black Beans, and 1/2 your Mexican Style Cheese
7. Add your last Tortilla on top of that layer, the rest of your mix, other 1/2 Black Beans, Salsa, and Mexican Style Cheese
8. Bake on 350F/176C for 25 minutes

$5.10   35:00

54

CHICKEN OR TUNA MELT BALLS

NUTRITION

Whole Recipe
Makes: 1 Recipe
Calories: 873
Fat: 25g
Saturated Fat: 2g
Sodium: 2551mg
Carbs: 67g
Fiber: 11g
Sugar: 9g
Protein: 95g

1 BALL
Makes: 9 Balls
Calories: 97
Fat: 2.7g
Saturated Fat: .2g
Sodium: 283.4mg
Carbs: 7.4g
Fiber: 1.2g
Sugar: 1g
Protein: 10.5g

INGREDIENTS

2 cans chicken or tuna
2 extra large eggs
1 cup (90g) whole wheat bread crumbs or wheat germ
2/3 cup reduced fat mild cheddar cheese or other cheese
1/4 teaspoon black pepper
1 teaspoon lemon juice
1 teaspoon parsley
4 tablespoons (60g) low fat mayonnaise
1/2 cup celery
1/4 cup red onion

HOW TO MAKE THEM

1. Drain your Chicken or Tuna, chop up your Celery and Red Onion, and combine all of your ingredients into a bowl
2. Mix everything together
3. Take out a baking sheet, coat it with some non-stick cooking spray, and shape your mix into balls
4. Bake on 350F/176C for 15-20 minutes

$3.40   20:00

TIPS

Top them with some sour cream or plain Greek yogurt!

Keep them in the fridge and they'll last around 5-7 days!

CHEESY LEAN BAKE

INGREDIENTS

- 2 cups (496g) fat free ricotta cheese
- 1 cup mushrooms
- 1 cup (112g) reduced fat cheddar cheese
- 4 ounces (112g) cooked pasta
- 8 tablespoons (40g) grated parmesan cheese
- 1 green bell pepper
- 1 teaspoon italian seasoning
- 2 pounds (32 ounces) cooked chicken or any other lean protein such as ground beef, turkey, tofu, etc
- 1/4 cup white onion
- 10 3/4 ounces (305g) 98% fat free cream of chicken
- 1/4 cup (28g) whole wheat bread crumbs

HOW TO MAKE IT

1. Chop up your Lean Protein, Mushrooms, Green Bell Pepper, and White Onion
2. Add all of your ingredients into a large bowl aside from your Bread Crumbs and mix everything together
3. Evenly distribute your mix into a baking dish
4. Top it with your Bread Crumbs
5. Bake on 350F/176C for 45 minutes or until the edges start to bubble

$6.60   45:00

TIP

Keep it in the frige and it'll usually last around 5-7 days!

NUTRITION

Whole Recipe
Makes: 1 Recipe
Calories: 2326
Fat: 46g
Saturated Fat: 12g
Sodium: 3041mg
Carbs: 179g
Fiber: 20g
Sugar: 29g
Protein: 299g

1 PLATE
Makes: 6 Plates
Calories: 387
Fat: 7.6g
Saturated Fat: 2g
Sodium: 506.8mg
Carbs: 29.8g
Fiber: 3.3g
Sugar: 4.8g
Protein: 49.8g

CHEESY LEAN MEATBALLS

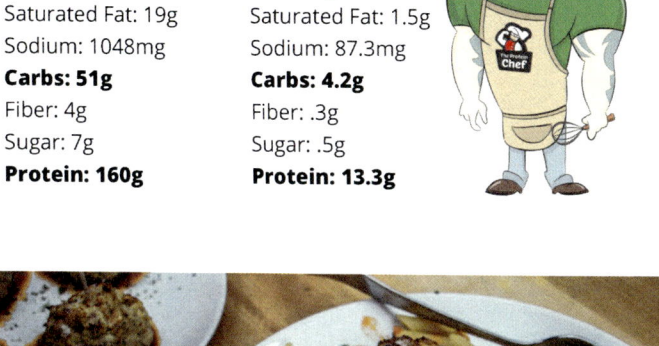

INGREDIENTS

- 1 pound (16 ounces) ground chicken, beef, or turkey
- 1 large egg or 2 large egg whites
- 3 ounces (84g) fat free cream cheese or cottage cheese
- 1/2 cup (56g) seasoned bread crumbs
- 8 tablespoons (40g) grated parmesan cheese
- 2 teaspoons minced garlic
- 1 tablespoon italian seasoning
- 1/2 teaspoon salt
- 1/2 teaspoon black pepper

HOW TO MAKE THEM

1. Combine all of your ingredients into a bowl
2. Mix everything together
3. Take out a baking sheet, coat it with some non-stick cooking spray, and shape your mix into balls
4. Put your balls into the oven on 450F/232C for 15-20 minutes

$3.75   20:00

TIPS

The leaner your protein is (I like 93/7 with this one) the less total fat the recipe will have!

Change your flavor up by adding in your favorite herbs, spices, and/or vegetables!

NUTRITION

Whole Recipe
Makes: 1 Recipe
Calories: 1438
Fat: 66g
Saturated Fat: 19g
Sodium: 1048mg
Carbs: 51g
Fiber: 4g
Sugar: 7g
Protein: 160g

1 MEATBALL
Makes: 12 MEATBALLS
Calories: 119
Fat: 5.5g
Saturated Fat: 1.5g
Sodium: 87.3mg
Carbs: 4.2g
Fiber: .3g
Sugar: .5g
Protein: 13.3g

INGREDIENTS

2 large eggs
2 teaspoons minced garlic
1/2 teaspoon onion powder
1/2 teaspoon chili powder
8 tablespoons (60g) parmesan cheese
2 cups (452g) fat free cottage cheese
1 cups chopped greens (kale or spinach work best)

HOW TO MAKE IT

1. Chop up your Greens and mix everything together in a large bowl
2. Add your mix into an oven safe dish
3. Bake on 350F/176C for 15-20 minutes or until the sides start to bubble

$2.70   20:00

TIPS

It tastes just as good cold so you can take it with you on the go!

Spice it up even more by adding in some chili sauce!

MORE TIPS

Double or triple the recipe to have enough for the whole week!

Eat it like a dip using some pita chips!

COTTAGE CHEESE CASSEROLE

NUTRITION

Whole Recipe
Makes: 1 Recipe
Calories: 776
Fat: 28g
Saturated Fat: 15g
Sodium: 935mg
Carbs: 35g
Fiber: 2g
Sugar: 14g
Protein: 96g

1 PLATE
Makes: 4 Plates
Calories: 194
Fat: 7g
Saturated Fat: 3.7g
Sodium: 233.7mg
Carbs: 8.7g
Fiber: .5g
Sugar: 3.5g
Protein: 24g

NUTRITION

Whole Recipe
Makes: 1 Recipe
Calories: 2898
Fat: 62g
Saturated Fat: 18g
Sodium: 2604mg
Carbs: 294g
Fiber: 54g
Sugar: 49g
Protein: 291g

1 BOWL
Makes: 6 Bowls
Calories: 483
Fat: 10.3g
Saturated Fat: 3g
Sodium: 434mg
Carbs: 49g
Fiber: 9g
Sugar: 8.1g
Protein: 48.5g

ENCHILADA PASTA

INGREDIENTS

2 cups (16 ounces) water
6 ounces (168g) whole wheat pasta
2 teaspoons chili powder
14.5 ounces (411g) no salt added diced tomatoes
10 ounces (283) low sodium enchilada sauce
15 ounces (425g) reduced sodium black beans
11 ounces (311g) no salt added whole kernel corn
2 pounds (32 ounces) cooked chicken breast or any other lean protein such as ground beef, turkey, tofu, etc
1 cup (112g) reduced fat cheddar cheese

HOW TO MAKE IT

1. Take out a large stove top pan and turn your burner on High Heat
2. Add in your Water, Pasta, Chili Powder, Diced Tomatoes, and Enchilada Sauce
3. Mix everything together and bring it to a boil
4. Once it starts to boil turn your burner down to Low-Medium Heat and let it simmer for 15 minutes while occasionally stirring it
5. After 15 minutes add in your Black Beans, Corn, and chopped up chicken or lean protein of your choice
6. Mix everything around and keep those ingredients on the heat for 3 minutes
7. After 3 minutes mix in your Cheese until it's melted

💲 **$7.50**   ⏱ **28:00**

TIP

Top your serving with some chopped green onions!

LEAN PARMESAN

INGREDIENTS

1 1/2 pounds (24 ounces) chicken or turkey breast
2 extra large egg whites
1 tablespoon olive oil
2/3 cup (60g) whole wheat bread crumbs
8 tablespoons (40g) grated parmesan cheese
1/2 cup (123g) pasta sauce
3/4 cup (84g) reduced fat mozzarella cheese

HOW TO MAKE IT

1. Take out your Chicken or Turkey Breast, trim the fat off of them, and cut them in half
2. In a small bowl add in your Egg Whites and Olive Oil
3. Mix those together
4. In a large bowl add in your Bread Crumbs and Parmesan Cheese
5. Mix those together
6. Take out a baking sheet, coat it with some non-stick cooking spray, and put your chicken or turkey onto your baking sheet
7. Lightly brush your wet mix onto both sides of each piece then dunk them into your dry mix
8. Coat the top of each piece with some non-stick cooking spray and put them into the oven on 450F/232C for 20 minutes
9. After 20 minutes take them out, flip them over, and evenly distribute your Pasta Sauce and Mozzarella Cheese over the top of them
10. Put them back into the oven on 450F/232C for another 5-10 minutes or until your cheese is melted

$4.00   30:00

NUTRITION

Whole Recipe
Makes: 1 Recipe
Calories: 1515
Fat: 43g
Saturated Fat: 14g
Sodium: 2010mg
Carbs: 55g
Fiber: 6g
Sugar: 10g
Protein: 227g

1 PLATE
Makes: 6 Plates
Calories: 252
Fat: 7.1g
Saturated Fat: 2.3g
Sodium: 335mg
Carbs: 9.1g
Fiber: 1g
Sugar: 1.6g
Protein: 37.8g

CRISPY COCONUT CHICKEN

INGREDIENTS

1 jumbo egg
1 tablespoon (14g) coconut oil
8 tablespoons (60g) coconut flour
8 tablespoons (60g) coconut flakes
2 pounds (32 ounces) chicken breast

TIPS

Reheat them using the toaster oven to keep the crispiness alive!

Using sweetened coconut flakes will net you a much more enjoyable taste!

Use a wire baking rack on top of your baking sheet to keep them from getting soggy!

HOW TO MAKE THEM

1. Take out 3 bowls and melt your Coconut Oil
2. Add your Egg and melted Coconut Oil into one bowl and mix those together
3. Add your Coconut Flour into the next bowl
4. Add your Coconut Flakes into the last bowl
5. Take out your Chicken Breast, trim the fat off of them, and cut them into strips (however big you want them)
6. Dunk your strips first into the Coconut Flour, then egg mix, and last the Coconut Flakes
7. Place your strips onto your baking sheet and bake them on 400F/204C for 15:00-20:00

$6.60   45:00

NUTRITION

Whole Recipe
Makes: 1 Recipe
Calories: 1705
Fat: 73g
Saturated Fat: 46g
Sodium: 1504mg
Carbs: 64g
Fiber: 28g
Sugar: 28g
Protein: 198g

1 PLATE
Makes: 10 Plates
Calories: 170
Fat: 7.3g
Saturated Fat: 4.6g
Sodium: 150.4mg
Carbs: 6.4g
Fiber: 2.8g
Sugar: 2.8g
Protein: 19.8g

FAJITA MEATLOAF

INGREDIENTS

2 pounds (32 ounces) 97% lean ground beef or turkey
2 large eggs
1/2 cup (40g) rolled oats
1.25 ounces (35g) low sodium fajita seasoning mix
1/2 cup (56g) reduced fat mexican blend cheese
1/4 teaspoon black pepper
1/2 cup red onion
1 yellow pepper
1 green pepper
10 tablespoons (150g) salsa

HOW TO MAKE IT

1. Chop up your Red Onion, Yellow Pepper, and Green Pepper
2. Add all of your ingredients into a large bowl and mix everything together
3. Take out at least a 9x5 pan, coat it with some non-stick cooking spray, and add your mix in
4. Put your meatloaf into the oven on 350F/176C for 1 hour
5. After 1 hour take it out and top it with your Salsa before cutting it

TIP

Can't find fajita seasoning mix? Make your own!

$7.60   60:00

NUTRITION

Whole Recipe
Makes: 1 Recipe
Calories: 1625
Fat: 37g
Saturated Fat: 12g
Sodium: 1298mg
Carbs: 79g
Fiber: 9g
Sugar: 20g
Protein: 244g

1 PIECE
Makes: 8 Pieces
Calories: 203
Fat: 4.6g
Saturated Fat: 1.5g
Sodium: 162.2mg
Carbs: 9.8g
Fiber: 1.1g
Sugar: 2.5g
Protein: 30.5g

HOLIDAY MEATBALLS

NUTRITION

Whole Recipe
Makes: 1 Recipe
Calories: 1540
Fat: 52g
Saturated Fat: 16g
Sodium: 1446mg
Carbs: 130g
Fiber: 5g
Sugar: 42g
Protein: 138g

1 MEATBALL
Makes: 12 Meatballs
Calories: 128
Fat: 4.3g
Saturated Fat: 1.3g
Sodium: 120.5mg
Carbs: 10.8g
Fiber: .4g
Sugar: 3.5g
Protein: 11.5g

INGREDIENTS

1.3 pounds (20.8 ounces) 93/7 lean ground beef, turkey, or chicken
2 large eggs
4 servings (112g) stuffing mix
2 tablespoons (34g) ketchup
1/4 teaspoon black pepper
1/4 teaspoon ground ginger
1/2 teaspoon garlic powder
1/4 cup (40g) craisins
1/4 cup red onion

HOW TO MAKE THEM

1. Chop up your Red Onion
2. Combine all of your ingredients into a bowl and mix them together
3. Take out a baking sheet, coat it with some non-stick cooking spray, and shape your mix into balls
4. Bake on 375F/190C for 25-30 minutes

💰 **$5.80** ⏱ **30:00**

TIPS

Serve them as an appetizer with some gravy or barbecue sauce!

These will last around 5-7 days and YES, you can freeze them!

Heat them up for around :10-:20 seconds a piece in the microwave!

LOW CARB CHICKEN FINGERS

INGREDIENTS

1 1/2 pounds (24 ounces) chicken or turkey breast
1 cup (112g) almond flour
1 teaspoon black pepper
1/2 teaspoon salt
1 teaspoon garlic powder
1 1/2 teaspoons chili pepper powder
2 large eggs
2 large egg whites

$3.50   25:00

HOW TO MAKE THEM

1. Take out a bowl, add in all of your dry ingredients, and mix those together
2. Take out another bowl, add your Eggs into it, and mix them up
3. Trim the fat off your Chicken Breast and cut them into whatever size chicken fingers you'd like
4. Take out a baking pan and coat it with some non-stick cooking spray
5. Dunk each piece of chicken into your egg mix then into your dry mix until fully coated and put it on your baking sheet
6. Evenly distribute any mix left over across the top of your chicken fingers
7. Bake on 375F/190C for 20-25 minutes

TIP

Use a wire baking rack on top of your baking sheet to keep them from getting soggy!

NUTRITION

Whole Recipe
Makes: 1 Recipe
Calories: 1531
Fat: 79g
Saturated Fat: 8g
Sodium: 670mg
Carbs: 24g
Fiber: 12g
Sugar: 4g
Protein: 181g

1 PLATE
Makes: 4 Plates
Calories: 382
Fat: 19.7g
Saturated Fat: 2g
Sodium: 167.5mg
Carbs: 6g
Fiber: 3g
Sugar: 1g
Protein: 45.2g

LOW CARB PIZZA

INGREDIENTS

crust
2 large eggs
4 large egg whites
6 ounces (180g) fat free cream cheese
1/4 cup (20g) rolled oats
3 tablespoons (15g) grated parmesan cheese
1 teaspoon italian seasoning

toppings
3/4 cup (189g) marinara
1/2 cup (56g) reduced fat pizza blend cheese
couple slices tomato

NUTRITION

Whole Recipe
Makes: 1 Recipe
Calories: 754
Fat: 30g
Saturated Fat: 12g
Sodium: 805mg
Carbs: 42g
Fiber: 4g
Sugar: 14g
Protein: 79g

1 PIECE
Makes: 4 Pieces
Calories: 188
Fat: 7.5g
Saturated Fat: 3g
Sodium: 201.2mg
Carbs: 10.5g
Fiber: 1g
Sugar: 3.5g
Protein: 19.7g

HOW TO MAKE IT

1. Turn your Rolled Oats into oat flour by processing or blending them until they look like flour
2. Add all of your ingredients for the crust into a bowl and mix them together until all of the chunks are gone
3. Take out a baking pan, coat it with some non-stick cooking spray, and pour your mix in
4. Make your pizza whatever shape you want it, just make sure to level out the top so that it bakes evenly
5. Bake on 375F/190C for 25 minutes
6. Remove your pizza and add your toppings
7. Put it back into the oven on 375F/190C for 10 minutes or until your cheese is melted

$1.50   35:00

SPICY CHICKEN OR TUNA CHILI

INGREDIENTS

2 tablespoons canola oil
2 14.4 ounce bags frozen pepper stir-fry vegetables
6 cans chicken or tuna
1.25 ounces (35g) chili seasoning mix
16 ounces (454g) reduced sodium dark red kidney beans or other beans
15 ounces (425g) reduced sodium black beans or other beans
10 tablespoons (165g) salsa
10 teaspoons (50g) chili sauce
28 ounces (794g) crushed tomatoes
2 teaspoons minced garlic

HOW TO MAKE IT

1. Drain and rinse your Dark Red Kidney and Black Beans
2. Drain your Chicken or Tuna
3. Take out a large stove top pan, turn your burner on Medium Heat, and add in your Canola Oil
4. Once your pan heats up add in your Pepper Stir-Fry and the rest of your ingredients while occasionally mixing everything around
5. Once all of your ingredients are in your pan and mixed together let your chili cook for 10-15 minutes, stirring it every couple of minutes

$10.10   20:00

TIP

This will last around 5 days in the fridge!

NUTRITION

Whole Recipe
Makes: 1 Recipe
Calories: 2280
Fat: 36g
Saturated Fat: 2g
Sodium: 4940mg
Carbs: 297g
Fiber: 76g
Sugar: 84g
Protein: 192g

1 BOWL
Makes: 6 Bowls
Calories: 380
Fat: 6g
Saturated Fat: .3g
Sodium: 823.3mg
Carbs: 49.5g
Fiber: 12.6g
Sugar: 14g
Protein: 32g

QUICK CHIPOTLE BURRITO BOWLS

INGREDIENTS

3 cups romaine
3/4 cup (105g) :90 second brown rice
1/2 cup (122g) reduced sodium black beans or other beans
1/2 cup (125g) whole kernel corn
1/4 cup (28g) reduced fat mexican blend cheese or other cheese
1/2 avocado
1/2 roma tomato
1/2 serving (14g) tortilla chips
3 tablespoons (45g) salsa
2.65 ounces (75g) fat free plain greek yogurt
1 teaspoon chili powder
1/2 teaspoon chipotle pepper
1 teaspoon minced garlic
couple squirts lime juice
8 ounces lean protein of your choice

HOW TO MAKE THEM

1. To make your dressing combine your Greek Yogurt, Chili Powder, Chipotle Pepper, and Minced Garlic together in a small bowl
2. Mix those ingredients together and put your dressing off to the side
3. Chop up your Roma Tomato and Avocado
4. Crush up your Tortilla Chips
5. Add the rest of your ingredients together in a large bowl
6. Portion it out into however many servings you want
7. Top your serving with some dressing

$3.50   10:00

NUTRITION

Whole Recipe
Makes: 1 Recipe
Calories: 1009
Fat: 33g
Saturated Fat: 10g
Sodium: 900mg
Carbs: 94g
Fiber: 20g
Sugar: 14g
Protein: 84g

1 BOWL
Makes: 2 Bowls
Calories: 504
Fat: 16.5g
Saturated Fat: 5g
Sodium: 450mg
Carbs: 47g
Fiber: 10g
Sugar: 7g
Protein: 42g

67

QUICK LEAN CHILI

INGREDIENTS

1 1/2 tablespoons olive oil
1.3 pounds (20.8 ounces) lean ground beef or turkey
2 cups (16 ounces) water
1/2 red onion
1 red bell pepper
1 1/2 teaspoons minced garlic
6 tablespoons (90g) diced green chiles
28 ounces (794g) crushed tomatoes
1 teaspoon crushed red pepper
15 ounces (425g) reduced sodium black beans or other beans
16 ounces (454g) reduced sodium dark red kidney beans or other beans
1.25 ounces (35g) chili seasoning mix

NUTRITION

Whole Recipe
Makes: 1 Recipe
Calories: 2317
Fat: 69g
Saturated Fat: 16g
Sodium: 3646mg
Carbs: 245g
Fiber: 55g
Sugar: 68g
Protein: 179g

1 BOWL
Makes: 10 Bowls
Calories: 231
Fat: 6.9g
Saturated Fat: 1.6g
Sodium: 364.6mg
Carbs: 24.5g
Fiber: 5.5g
Sugar: 6.8g
Protein: 17.9g

$5.50   45:00

HOW TO MAKE IT

1. Take out a large stove top pan, turn your burner on Medium Heat, and add in your Olive Oil
2. Once your pan heats up add in your Beef or Turkey and brown it
3. Chop up your Red Onion and Bell Pepper
4. After your Beef or Turkey has browned add in the rest of your ingredients while occasionally mixing everything together
5. Bring your chili to a boil, cover it, turn your burner on Low Heat, and let it simmer for 30-35 minutes

SLOW COOKED LEAN POT PIE

INGREDIENTS

5 pounds (80 ounces) chicken breast or any other lean protein such as ground beef, turkey, tofu, etc
32 1/4 ounces (915g) fat free cream of chicken
10 3/4 ounces (305g) 98% fat free cream of celery
10 3/4 ounces (305g) 98% fat free cream of mushroom
1 1/2 teaspoons black pepper
1 teaspoon garlic salt
1 teaspoon onion powder
5 packets or cubes no sodium chicken bouillon
1 1/2 cups sliced mushrooms
1 cup chopped celery
1 cup chopped carrots
16 ounces (453g) frozen mixed vegetables
8 red potatoes

HOW TO MAKE IT

1. Take out your Chicken Breast or lean protein of your choice, trim the fat off of them, and cut them in half
2. Chop up your Celery, Carrots, and Red Potatoes
3. Combine all of your ingredients into your slow cooker
4. Mix everything together
5. Cook on High Heat for 5-6 hours

$13.45   6 Hours

TIP

Top your pot pie with some bread crumbs!

NUTRITION

Whole Recipe
Makes: 1 Recipe
Calories: 4939
Fat: 47g
Saturated Fat: 10g
Sodium: 6504mg
Carbs: 439g
Fiber: 61g
Sugar: 70g
Protein: 690g

1 BOWL
Makes: 10 Bowls
Calories: 493
Fat: 4.7g
Saturated Fat: 1g
Sodium: 650mg
Carbs: 43.9g
Fiber: 6.1g
Sugar: 7g
Protein: 69g

ALL OF THE...
SIDE RECIPES

INGREDIENTS

1 head fresh cauliflower
3 cloves garlic
2 tablespoons parsley
1 tablespoon butter
1/2 teaspoon salt
1/2 teaspoon black pepper
1 ounce fat free milk or milk substitute

$1.50   30:00

HOW TO MAKE THEM

1. Cook your Cauliflower
2. Combine all of your ingredients into a food processor
3. Process everything together until it looks like mashed potatoes

TIPS

Fresh cauliflower will work much better than frozen cauliflower!

Add herbs or spices to change up the flavor!

CAULIFLOWER MASHED

NUTRITION

Whole Recipe
Makes: 1 Recipe
Calories: 296
Fat: 12g
Saturated Fat: 7g
Sodium: 280mg
Carbs: 34g
Fiber: 15g
Sugar: 16g
Protein: 13g

1 BOWL
Makes: 2 Bowls
Calories: 148
Fat: 6g
Saturated Fat: 3.5g
Sodium: 140mg
Carbs: 17g
Fiber: 7.5g
Sugar: 8g
Protein: 6.5g

LOW CARB LASAGNA DIP

INGREDIENTS

1 pound (16 ounces) lean ground beef, chicken, pork, turkey, etc
1 tablespoon olive oil
2 cups (488g) no salt added crushed tomatoes
4 tablespoon (66g) no salt added tomato paste
1 1/2 teaspoons minced garlic
1/4 cup red onion
1 1/2 cups (339g) fat free cottage cheese
1 1/2 cups (168g) reduced fat mozzarella cheese

NUTRITION

Whole Recipe
Makes: 1 Recipe
Calories: 1600
Fat: 60g
Saturated Fat: 21g
Sodium: 1710mg
Carbs: 76g
Fiber: 9g
Sugar: 37g
Protein: 189g

1 BOWL
Makes: 10 Bowls
Calories: 160
Fat: 6g
Saturated Fat: 2.1g
Sodium: 171mg
Carbs: 7.6g
Fiber: .9g
Sugar: 3.7g
Protein: 18.9g

HOW TO MAKE IT

1. Take out a large stove top pan and brown your choice of meat
2. Once browned add in the rest of your ingredients aside from your Cottage Cheese and Mozzarella
3. Mix everything together and let it simmer on Low Heat for 10 minutes
4. Take out a baking dish or pan and add your Cottage Cheese to the bottom of it
5. Pour your mix on top of your Cottage Cheese
6. Top your dish or pan with your Mozzarella then bake on 350F/176C for 15-20 minutes

$3.50   35:00

LOW FAT HUMMUS

INGREDIENTS

16 ounces (454g) reduced sodium chickpeas
2 tablespoons olive oil
1/2 teaspoon ground cumin
1 teaspoon salt
pinch black pepper
1 tablespoon lemon juice
4 cloves (2 teaspoons) minced garlic
3 ounces (85g) fat free plain greek yogurt

HOW TO MAKE IT

1. Drain and rinse your Chickpeas
2. Mince your Garlic
3. Add all of your ingredients into either a food processor or really powerful blender
4. Process or blend everything together for around :30 seconds or until it starts to look like hummus

💰 **$1.20**   ⏱ **2:00**

TIPS

Make this recipe high protein by adding in some unflavored or vanilla protein powder!

Want it spicy? Add in some chili sauce and/or crushed red pepper!

Add in chopped vegetables, nuts, or anything else you like in your hummus!

NUTRITION

Whole Recipe
Makes: 1 Recipe
Calories: 717
Fat: 29g
Saturated Fat: 4g
Sodium: 480mg
Carbs: 76g
Fiber: 25g
Sugar: 6g
Protein: 38g

PROTEIN CORNBREAD

INGREDIENTS

1/4 cup (2 ounces) fat free milk or milk substitute
1 large egg or 2 large egg whites
1/4 cup (61g) unsweetened apple sauce
1 cup (8 ounces) fat free plain greek yogurt
1 tablespoon (21g) honey
1/4 cup (20g) rolled oats
3/4 cup (99g) cornmeal
1/2 teaspoon salt
1 scoop (30g) unflavored protein powder
2 teaspoons baking powder
1/4 teaspoon baking soda

NUTRITION

Whole Recipe
Makes: 1 Recipe
Calories: 818
Fat: 10g
Saturated Fat: 2g
Sodium: 375mg
Carbs: 120g
Fiber: 18g
Sugar: 33g
Protein: 62g

1 PIECE
Makes: 10 Pieces
Calories: 81
Fat: 1g
Saturated Fat: .2g
Sodium: 37.5mg
Carbs: 12g
Fiber: 1.8g
Sugar: 3.3g
Protein: 6.2g

HOW TO MAKE IT

1. Turn your Rolled Oats into oat flour by blending or processing them until they look like flour
2. Mix all of the ingredients together in a bowl
3. Coat a 9x7 or 8x8 baking dish with some non-stick cooking spray
4. Pour mix into the baking dish
5. Bake on 425F/218C for 15-20 minutes

$1.85   20:00

TIP

Use a vanilla protein powder if you want them to taste a bit sweeter!

SPICY 7 LAYER DIP

INGREDIENTS

2 cans chicken, tuna, or tofu
8 tablespoons (36g) taco seasoning mix
10.6 ounces (300g) fat free plain greek yogurt
3 teaspoons (15g) chili sauce
1/2 teaspoon crushed red pepper
7 tablespoons (108.5g) guacamole
1/2 cup (56g) reduced fat mexican cheese or other cheese
16 ounces (454g) reduced sodium pinto beans or any other beans
1/4 cup (2 ounces) water
10 tablespoons (165g) salsa

HOW TO MAKE IT

1. Drain your Chicken or Tuna
2. Add in your Chicken, Tuna, or Tofu, 1/2 your Greek Yogurt, 1/2 your Taco Seasoning Mix, and your Chili Sauce
3. Mix all of those ingredients together
4. Take out another bowl and add in your mix as your first layer
5. On top of that layer add your Mexican Cheese
6. Drain and rinse your Pinto Beans
7. Put them in a separate bowl with your other 1/2 Taco Seasoning Mix and Water
8. Mix all of those ingredients together while mashing your Pinto Beans up
9. Microwave your Pinto Bean mix for :45 seconds and add your Pinto Bean mix on top of your Mexican Cheese layer
10. Spread your Guacamole over that layer
11. On top of that add the other 1/2 of your Greek Yogurt
12. Add your Salsa

$3.85 **45:00**

TIP

Top it with some Black Olive Slices, Green Onion, and a couple squirts of Chili Sauce!

NUTRITION

Whole Recipe
Makes: 1 Recipe
Calories: 1299
Fat: 31g
Saturated Fat: 9g
Sodium: 3210mg
Carbs: 128g
Fiber: 32g
Sugar: 23g
Protein: 127g

1 BOWL
Makes: 10 Bowls
Calories: 129
Fat: 3.1g
Saturated Fat: .9g
Sodium: 321mg
Carbs: 12.8g
Fiber: 3.2g
Sugar: 2.3g
Protein: 12.7g

TUNA OR CHICKEN SALAD

INGREDIENTS

2 cans chicken or tuna
1 tablespoon (15g) no sugar added sweet relish
pinch black pepper
1 teaspoon parsley
2 tablespoons (14g) bacon bits
1/2 teaspoon lemon juice
1/4 cup red onion
1/4 cup celery
5.3 ounces (150g) fat free plain greek yogurt
2 large hard boiled eggs

NUTRITION

Whole Recipe
Makes: 1 Recipe
Calories: 577
Fat: 21g
Saturated Fat: 5g
Sodium: 743mg
Carbs: 13g
Fiber: 2g
Sugar: 7g
Protein: 84g

1 BOWL
Makes: 2 Bowls
Calories: 288
Fat: 10.5g
Saturated Fat: 2.5g
Sodium: 371.5mg
Carbs: 6.5g
Fiber: 1g
Sugar: 3.5g
Protein: 42g

HOW TO MAKE IT

1. Hard boil 2 Large Eggs
2. Chop up your Hard Boiled Eggs, Red Onion, and Celery
3. Combine all of your ingredients into a bowl
4. Mix everything together.

$2.25   5:00

TIP

Make it spicy by adding in a little chili sauce!

TUNA PANCAKES

INGREDIENTS

1/2 cup (40g) rolled oats
2 cans tuna
1/2 teaspoon black pepper
1/4 teaspoon salt
1 1/2 teaspoons minced garlic
2 large eggs
1/4 cup red onion
2 tablespoons canola oil

HOW TO MAKE THEM

1. Blend or process your Rolled Oats until they look like flour
2. Drain your Tuna, chop up your Red Onion, and combine all of your ingredients into a bowl aside from your Canola Oil
3. Mix everything together
4. Take out a stove top pan, put your burner on Medium Heat, add your Canola Oil into your stove top pan, and let that heat up
5. Shape your mix into pancakes, however big you want to make them, and cook each side for around 2-3 minutes or until they are golden brown

$3.40   12:00

TIPS

Double or triple your recipe to last you the whole day!

Add spices, chili sauce, barbecue sauce, soy sauce, or anything else you can think of into the recipe or on top of them!

NUTRITION

Whole Recipe
Makes: 1 Recipe
Calories: 625
Fat: 29g
Saturated Fat: 5g
Sodium: 861mg
Carbs: 30g
Fiber: 4g
Sugar: 2g
Protein: 61g

The Protein Chef

Made in the USA
Columbia, SC
30 October 2020